E–H

Ecuadoreans to Haitians

Titles in the series

A–D
Afghans to Dominicans

E–H
Ecuadoreans to Haitians

I–L
Indians to Laotians

M–P
Mexicans to Puerto Ricans

R–V
Russians to Vietnamese

The NEWEST Americans

E–H
Ecuadoreans to Haitians

GREENWOOD PRESS
Westport, Connecticut · London

Library of Congress Cataloging-in-Publication Data

Creative Media Applications
  The newest Americans
      p. cm.–(Middle school reference)
  Includes bibliographical references and index.
  ISBN 0-313-32553-7 (set: alk. paper)–0-313-32554-5 (v.1)–0-313-32555-3 (v.2)–
  0-313-32556-1 (v.3)–0-313-32557-X (v.4)–0-313-32563-4 (v.5)
    1. Immigrants–United States–Juvenile literature–Encyclopedias.
    2. United States–Emigration and immigration–Juvenile literature–Encyclopedias.
    3. Minorities–United States–Juvenile literature–Encyclopedias.
    [1. Immigrants–United States–Encyclopedias. 2. United States–Emigration and
    immigration–Encyclopedias. 3. Minorities–Encyclopedias.] I. Series.
  JV6455.N48 2003
  304.8'73'03–dc21   2002035214

British Library Cataloguing in Publication Data is available.

Library of Congress Catalog Card Number: 2002035214
ISBN: 0–313–32553–7 (set)
           0–313–32554–5 (vol. 1)
           0–313–32555–3 (vol. 2)
           0–313–32556–1 (vol. 3)
           0–313–32557–X (vol. 4)
           0–313–32563–4 (vol. 5)

First published in 2003

Greenwood Press, 88 Post Road West, Westport, CT 06881
An imprint of Greenwood Publishing Group, Inc.
www.greenwood.com

Printed in the United States of America

The paper used in this book complies with the Permanent Paper Standard issued by the
National Information Standards Organization (Z39.48–1984).

10 9 8 7 6 5 4 3 2 1

A Creative Media Applications, Inc. Production
WRITER: Sandy Pobst
DESIGN AND PRODUCTION: Fabia Wargin Design, Inc.
EDITOR: Susan Madoff
COPYEDITOR: Laurie Lieb
PROOFREADER: Betty Pessagno
INDEXER: Nara Wood
ASSOCIATED PRESS PHOTO RESEARCHER: Yvette Reyes
CONSULTANT: Robert Asher, University of Connecticut

Special thanks to Michaelle Vincent, District Supervisor for Haitian-Creole Language
Programs, Miami-Dade County Public Schools for her contributions to the Haitian chapter.

PHOTO CREDITS:
Cover: © Kim Kulish/CORBIS SABA
AP/Wide World Photographs *pages* 6, 19, 25, 28, 35, 39, 40, 45, 48, 53, 58, 65, 66, 69, 71, 74,
76, 77, 83, 85, 89, 91, 95, 96, 97, 101, 107, 115, 117, 123, 124, 129, 131, 134
© Kim Kulish/CORBIS SABA *page* 14
© Owen Franken/CORBIS *pages* 31, 86
© Pablo Corral V/CORBIS *page* 32
© James A Sugar/CORBIS *page* 50
© CORBIS *pages* 55, 60, 121
© Liba Taylor/CORBIS *page* 87
©Bettmann/CORBIS *page* 93
©Buddy May/CORBIS *page*s 103, 110

Contents

—Ralph Waldo Emerson

A Word about
The Newest Americans

This series takes a look at the people who have been coming to America from 1965 to the present. It provides historical, social, political, and cultural information on the most recent immigrant groups that are changing the face of America.

Charts and graphs show how immigration has been affected over the years, both by changes in the U.S. laws and by events in the sending country. Unless otherwise noted, the term *immigrant* in this book, including the charts and graphs, refers to new legal immigrants and to refugees and asylees who have changed their status to legal permanent residents.

From its very beginning, the United States stood for opportunity and freedom. It exists because immigrants, people who moved from their homes to make a new life in a new country, dreamed of better lives. They dreamed of having a voice in their government, of expressing their opinions and practicing their religion without fear of being imprisoned or tortured. Two hundred years later, these dreams still call to people around the world.

opposite:
A recent immigrant to the United States, the popular singer and songwriter Shakira is a blend of nationalities. Her mother is Colombian, and her father was born in Lebanon.

An Immigrant Nation

America declared its independence from British rule in 1776. At that time, nearly 80 percent of the people living in the colonies were white Europeans from England, Ireland, Scotland, Germany, the Netherlands, France, and Sweden. Just over 20 percent were slaves from Africa, the one group of American immigrants who did not come to this country willingly.

Over the next 200 years, more than 70 million people from around the world would *immigrate* to the United States. The majority came for *economic* reasons, eager to make the American dream a reality. Although this was one of the largest migrations of people in history, it began slowly. Wars in the United States and Europe kept immigration to a minimum until the 1820s. As things became more settled, however, a rapidly growing population that had few opportunities in Europe looked once more to America.

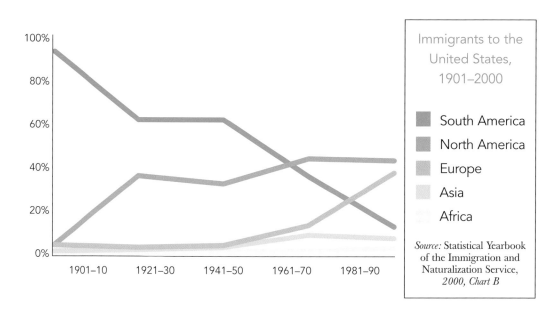

Immigrants to the United States, 1901–2000

- South America
- North America
- Europe
- Asia
- Africa

Source: Statistical Yearbook of the Immigration and Naturalization Service, *2000, Chart B*

—Motto of the United States

The 1800s

America offered freedom and political equality, but it also had practical attractions. Vast amounts of land unclaimed by white settlers, coupled with a growing number of jobs in the United States, exerted a strong pull on the imagination. Immigrants believed that they could improve their lives—and maybe even become wealthy—if they could only get to America.

There were many factors "pushing" immigrants to the United States as well. Population explosions, poor economic conditions, and widespread famine in Europe left many without work during the 1830s and 1840s.

The next big wave of immigrants reached American shores in the 1880s and 1890s. This time the newcomers included large numbers of southern and eastern Europeans. Immigrants from Italy, Austria-Hungary, Russia, and Poland began settling in America's cities and working in the factories.

Immigrant Chains

Immigrant chains form when members of one immigrant family settle in America, and then convince family members and friends to join them. The established immigrants help the new immigrants find homes and work in the same area. Immigrant chains have influenced settlement patterns all over the country, helping to create large communities of Cubans in Miami, Dominicans in New York, and Chinese in San Francisco, among others.

The 1900s

Immigration to the United States set a record in the first decade of the twentieth century. Nearly 9 million immigrants were recorded as entering the United States from 1901 to 1910.

For the first time, immigrants from southern and eastern Europe were in the majority. Many of these immigrants were Jewish and Catholic, in contrast to the predominantly Protestant groups that settled the United States. Immigration surged again from 1918 through 1921. Only when Congress enacted a quota system in 1921 and 1924 did immigration begin to decline. The *quota* system severely restricted the number of immigrants that would be allowed to enter the United States from each foreign country.

Immigration numbers remained low until the mid-1960s. But two events in particular caused America to rethink an immigration policy based on race and ethnicity. The first event was the *genocide* (systematic destruction) of European Jews during World War II. German leader Adolf Hitler's vision of a racially pure world was in direct opposition to the ideals the United States was based on. Yet the immigration policy was set up to admit primarily white Europeans. The second event was the American civil rights movement, which began in the mid-1950s and gained momentum in the 1960s. Many people felt that the United States, as a world leader, should adopt an immigration policy that would reflect its ideals of equality and freedom for everyone regardless of race or country of origin.

The Immigration and Nationality Act of 1965 introduced far-reaching changes in American immigration policy. The quota system was discarded in favor of worldwide limits. With family reunification as a priority, lawmakers allowed immediate family members of U.S. citizens to be admitted without limit.

Terrorist acts against the United States in 1993 and 2001 sparked changes to the immigration policy once again. The location of temporary (nonimmigrant) visitors, including students and businesspeople, is now being tracked more closely. The government has more freedom to investigate and detain suspected terrorists.

Immigration Today

In 2000, nearly 850,000 people became legal immigrants. Legal immigrants, also called legal permanent residents, receive paperwork, or documentation, that shows they are living in the United States legally. The documentation, commonly called a "green card," also allows a new permanent resident to work in the United States.

American immigration laws determine how many foreigners, or aliens, can enter the United States each year. Currently, the law allows between 421,000 and 675,000 immigrants to be admitted each year. Most of the yearly admissions are reserved for family-sponsored immigrants (up to 480,000 per year). People who have job skills that are in demand, such as scientists, software programmers, and computer analysts, are also among the first chosen. They qualify for the employment-based preferences (up to 140,000 per year).

Each year, 50,000 to 55,000 immigrants enter the United States through the Diversity Program. This program addresses the inequalities of past immigration policies. Residents of countries that have sent fewer than 50,000 immigrants to the United States in each of the past five years are eligible to participate. Visas, or permits, are issued to those applicants whose names are randomly selected, giving the program its common name—the diversity lottery.

Immigration Legislation

Until the late 1800s, there were few federal restrictions on immigration. States had the ability to control or limit immigration. This changed in 1875 when the federal government gained control of immigration. Beginning in the 1920s, the laws also specified the number of immigrants that could come to the United States each year.

Here is a brief description of the laws that have changed American immigration patterns over the past 200 years:

1882   The *Chinese Exclusion Act* stopped nearly all new immigration from China. Chinese immigrants would not be admitted in large numbers again until the 1950s.

1907   The so-called *Gentlemen's Agreement* blocked most Japanese immigration. A presidential order kept Hawaiian Japanese from moving to the United States.

1917   The *1917 Immigration Act* required immigrants to pass a literacy test before entering the United States. It also created a zone covering most of Asia. No immigration from this zone was allowed.

Immigrant Admissions in 2000

a	Immediate relative of U.S. citizen	41%
b	Family preference	28%
c	Employment preference	13%
d	Refugee/asylee adjustment	8%
e	Diversity Program	6%
f	Other	4%

Source: *Immigration and Naturalization Service*

1921   The *Quota Act* temporarily limited immigration after World War I. Immigration limits were based on national origin. Immigrants from the Western Hemisphere were not subject to limits.

1924   The *1924 Immigration Act* established the first permanent limits on immigration, continuing the national origins quota system. Before this law was enacted, the idea of illegal immigration did not exist.

1952   The *Immigration and Nationality Act of 1952* lifted some of the restrictions on Asian countries. Discrimination based on gender was eliminated. For the first time, preference was given to foreigners whose skills were in demand and to relatives of U.S. citizens and residents. Race-based limits were abolished when all races became eligible for naturalization.

1965   The groundbreaking *Immigration and Nationality Act of 1965* (also known as the Hart-Cellar Act) eliminated the quota system for worldwide limits.

1980   The *Refugee Act of 1980* established procedures for admitting and resettling *refugees*. It also made a distinction between refugees and asylees.

1986   The *Immigration Reform and Control Act (IRCA)* attempted to address the problem of illegal immigration. It provided an opportunity for immigrants who were living and working illegally in the United States before January 1, 1982, to adjust their status and eventually become legal residents and naturalized citizens.

1990   The *Immigration Act of 1990* made several major changes in U.S. policy. The total number of immigrants and refugees allowed to enter the United States each year increased dramatically. A Diversity Program allowed immigrants from countries that were underrepresented in America in the past an extra chance to receive a visa.

1996   The *Antiterrorism and Effective Death Penalty Act* outlined measures to identify and remove terrorists from the United States. It allowed the U.S. government to use evidence collected in secret to accuse immigrants of terrorist acts.

1996   The *Welfare Reform Act* was designed to keep most legal immigrants from getting food stamps and supplemental security income provided by the federal government.

1996   The *Illegal Immigration Reform and Immigrant Responsibility Act* focused on improving control of the U.S. borders.

2001   The *U.S.A. Patriot Act* expanded the government's ability to investigate, arrest, and deport legal residents for failing to comply with immigration regulations. Immigrants (including legal residents) who were suspected of terrorism could now be held indefinitely in detention centers.

Refugees and Asylees

Some people have to leave their countries because it isn't safe to live there anymore. Those who are afraid to return to their country because of persecution ask countries like the United States to take them in. People who are living outside the United States when they apply for protection are called refugees. They often have to wait years before their application is granted. The number of refugees permitted to resettle in the United States each year is determined by the president after discussions with Congress.

Like refugees, asylees are also seeking *asylum,* or safety from persecution. The difference is that asylees make their way to the United States before they ask for asylum. Most asylees come from countries that are located near the United States, such as Cuba, Nicaragua, and Guatemala.

Illegal Immigrants

In addition to the nearly 1 million legal immigrants who arrive in the United States each year, hundreds of thousands of people enter the country without permission. No one really knows how many illegal immigrants enter the United States each year. The Immigration and Naturalization Service (INS) estimates the number at close to 300,000 per year. These immigrants don't have the papers (visas) that show they have been admitted legally to the United States. They are often referred to as undocumented aliens or illegal immigrants.

In 1996, the INS estimated that 5 million undocumented immigrants were living in the United States. Today, experts suggest that the number is between 6 and 9 million. Over half are from Mexico. Because it is easier for people from nearby countries to enter the United States illegally, eight of the top ten countries sending illegal immigrants are in Central America, the Caribbean, and North America. The other two are the Philippines and Poland.

A group of new Americans take the oath of citizenship at the Los Angeles convention center.

Becoming Naturalized Citizens

American citizens enjoy many rights that permanent residents and visitors do not have. American citizens have the right to vote to select their leaders. They may hold government jobs and run for elected office. They can ask the government to allow family members to come to live in the United States. American citizens can also apply for a U.S. passport, making it easier to travel abroad.

Anyone who is born in the United States is automatically a citizen. Immigrants who want to become citizens must go through a process called naturalization. Before permanent residents can become naturalized citizens, they must live in the United States for a specified amount of time, usually three to five years. Once the residency requirement has been met, the resident must submit an application to the INS. A criminal check is completed during the application process.

The next step is an interview between the applicant and an INS officer. The ability to speak English is judged throughout the interview. Questions about the history and government of the United States test the immigrant's understanding of American civics. At the end of the interview, the officer either approves or denies the application for citizenship. An applicant who fails one of the tests may be given a second chance to pass the test.

Applicants who successfully complete the naturalization process attend a naturalization ceremony at which they swear an oath of allegiance to the United States. Each new citizen then receives a Certificate of Naturalization. Children under eighteen automatically become citizens when their parents take the oath of allegiance.

American Attitudes toward Immigration

Throughout America's history, immigrants have been both welcomed and feared. Negative attitudes toward immigrants tend to increase when the economy is in a slump. Increased competition for jobs and fears for the future lead many Americans to close ranks.

Discrimination

From the start, immigrants faced *discrimination* in America regardless of their race. Irish-Catholic, Japanese, Chinese, and Filipino immigrants have all been targets of hostility through the years.

Immigrants today continue to struggle to fit in. They are judged by their ability to speak English, their skin color, their clothing. Immigrant children comment that their new English vocabulary includes words like "discrimination," "prejudice," and "stereotype."

Immigration Myths and Realities

The debate over immigration has been heated from time to time. Amazingly, the same arguments against immigration have been made for over 100 years. Below are some of the claims that are often made about immigrants. The facts are also given.

Myth	*Reality*
Immigrants take jobs away from Americans.	New immigrants usually accept low-paying jobs that Americans don't want or won't accept. Immigrants often revitalize urban areas. Many open new businesses, providing jobs for others.
There are too many immigrants today. They outnumber Americans.	The actual number of immigrants in recent years does exceed that of past years. Immigrants in the 1990s, however, made up less than 3 percent of the population, compared to 9.6 percent from 1901 to 1910.
Immigrants come to America because they want to receive financial assistance, called welfare, from the government.	New immigrants must prove that they won't be a burden before they are allowed to enter the United States. Historically, new immigrants are more likely to be employed, save more of their earnings, and are more likely to start new businesses than native-born Americans. Recently, however, the percentage of immigrants receiving welfare is nearing that of native-born Americans.
Immigrants keep to themselves and speak their own languages. They don't want to be Americans.	Immigrants know that English is the key to success in the United States. Classes teaching English as a second language fill up quickly. There is usually a waiting list. Studies show that children of immigrants actually prefer English.
There is too much diversity among immigrants today. *Ethnic* enclaves, or communities, mean that immigrants don't have to adapt to the U.S. *culture*.	Some social scientists argue that *ethnic* enclaves form when immigration is not diverse enough.

The Immigrant Experience

Destinations

All immigrants to the United States have to make life-altering decisions that will change the course of their future. Their decisions are usually based on three main factors: location of family members, if any; opportunities for work; and proximity, or closeness, to their home country. These three factors have influenced settlement patterns since immigrants first began arriving on America's shores.

Although immigrants can live anywhere in the United States, nearly two-thirds of them settle in just six states. California, New York, Florida, Texas, New Jersey, and Illinois count more immigrants among their population than all other states combined. California alone is the destination of one-fourth of the nation's immigrants.

Because finding work and living near others who share their experience is so important, nearly all new immigrants (93 percent) live in urban areas. The most popular U.S. destinations in 2000 were New York City, Los Angeles, Miami, Chicago, and Washington, D.C.

Refugees do not necessarily follow these same settlement patterns, at least when they first arrive. As part of their relocation package, they are resettled into communities across the United States. Individuals or families in that community *sponsor* the refugees, helping them get used to their new surroundings. When refugees adjust their status to immigrant, they often choose to move to a location with a larger immigrant community.

Immigrant Destinations

a	California	25.6%
b	New York	12.5%
c	Florida	11.6%
d	Texas	7.5%
e	New Jersey	4.7%
f	Illinois	4.3%
g	All other states	33.8%

Source: Immigration and Naturalization Service

Fitting In

Social scientists call the process of adapting to a new culture *assimilation*. Assimilation takes place over time and in different ways. There is economic assimilation, in which immigrants take advantage of workplace opportunities to increase their income. Social and cultural assimilation take place as immigrants form friendships with Americans at school and at work. English skills improve and cultural traditions from their home country may be adapted. Young people especially become immersed in the American culture and begin to adopt those values. Finally, there is political assimilation. This occurs when immigrants choose to complete the naturalization process so their voices can be heard in their government.

CHAPTER ONE

Ecuadoreans

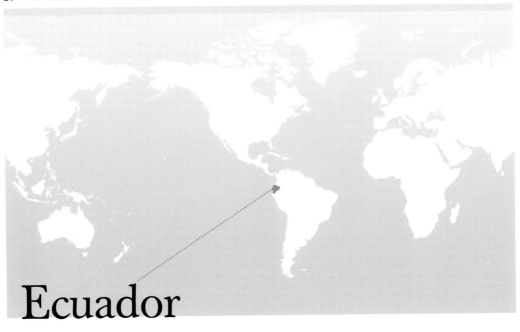

Ecuador

is one of South America's smallest countries. The name "Ecuador" is also the Spanish word for "equator." The equator is an imaginary line that divides our world into two parts, the Northern Hemisphere and the Southern Hemisphere. That line also runs through Ecuador.

The Andes Mountains run from north to south, dividing Ecuador into three major regions: the coastal plains, the highlands, and the eastern jungle. The people living in these regions reflect Ecuador's history of *conquerors* and freedom fighters. *Descendants* of the *Amerindians,* or native people, who first settled Ecuador as well as descendants of the Incas who conquered them, still live throughout the country, including the jungles in eastern Ecuador. Spanish conquerors opened Ecuador for colonization. Descendants of the Spanish colonists settled primarily along the coast. The mestizos, people with both Amerindian and Spanish *ancestors,* live in the coastal and highland regions. A small number of Ecuadoreans have European or African ancestors.

Ecuador's
Ethnic Groups

a Mestizo 44%

b Amerindian 25%

c European Descent 10%

d African Descent 8%

e Other 13%

*Source: Embassy of Ecuador
www.ecuador.org*

A Quick Look Back

Thousands of years ago, Ecuador was settled by several groups of Amerindians, including relatives of the Mayans (MY-ens) of Central America. One Amerindian empire, the kingdom of Quito (KEE-toe), stretched over much of present-day Ecuador. The fortified city of Quito that stood at the center of the kingdom is one of the oldest cities in North and South America. Today, Quito is the capital of Ecuador.

In the late 1400s, the Incas (INK-uhs) from Peru invaded and conquered the kingdom of Quito. It remained part of the Inca Empire, one of the most advanced *civilizations* of its time, until the Spanish conquerors defeated the Incas in 1534.

Spanish colonists were given ownership of large pieces of land by the Spanish government. In return, the settlers were expected to provide food and shelter for the native people living on their land, convert them to Roman Catholicism, and collect taxes from them. In reality, most of the settlers forced the native people to work as virtual slaves, often without providing the basic necessities. Thousands died from diseases passed along by the Spanish. Others escaped and began new lives in the jungle regions that the Spanish hadn't yet explored.

Gran Colombia

Ecuador was a Spanish colony for nearly 300 years. In the early 1800s, Ecuadoreans began to fight for their independence. At that time, Simón Bolívar, one of South America's greatest generals, was leading a revolution in Colombia, Panama, and Venezuela. When independence was won, the three countries united to create Gran Colombia. Bolívar then sent troops to Ecuador to help in its fight against Spain. Ecuador finally won its independence in 1822 and joined the other three countries in the Gran Colombia federation, or group.

Each country sent representatives to govern the Gran Colombia federation. They chose Bolívar as the first president, but he later declared himself a dictator. People became increasingly unhappy with Bolívar's government. Gran Colombia began to dissolve in 1829 when Venezuela withdrew from the federation. Ecuador soon followed.

Independence

In 1830, Ecuador became an independent country. Over the next fifteen years, the government introduced reforms and built schools and hospitals. The second president, Vincente Rocafuerte, developed strong ties with the countries around Ecuador. In the late 1800s, Ecuador's development surged ahead. Under the leadership of the Conservatives, roads were built and modern farming methods were introduced. The *economy* grew due to the demand for Ecuador's coffee, chocolate, and other agricultural products. However, the power and wealth remained concentrated in the hands of a relatively small group of land and business owners.

The Roman Catholic Church gained power during this period as well. Ecuador's constitution was amended in 1861 to make Roman Catholicism the official religion. Then, in 1869, citizenship became dependent upon whether one was a Roman Catholic. The Catholic Church was given the sole authority to develop and run Ecuador's schools.

The 1900s

Unlike the Conservatives, the Liberals wanted a clear division between the government and the Roman Catholic Church. They also wanted to improve the transportation and education systems. In 1895, the Liberals forcibly took control of the government. Under their leadership, Ecuador established a public education system. A railroad was built between Guayaquil (GWI-keel) and Quito, the two major cities.

By the 1920s, Ecuador added bananas to the list of agricultural products it was exporting. Soon most of the bananas sold in the world came from Ecuador. When the Great Depression hit the United States in 1929, many Americans lost their jobs and their homes. Americans couldn't afford the most basic necessities, let alone luxuries such as bananas, chocolate, and coffee. The economic hardship in the United States spread to countries that sold these types of products, including Ecuador.

Civil war and political instability marked the two decades that followed. The military led *coups* (kooz), or attacks, that forced elected presidents from office. The presidents were replaced by military dictators who ruled until they were overthrown. During the 1930s alone, Ecuador had fourteen presidents.

When World War II began, Ecuador sent troops to fight with the Allied forces. While the army was occupied, Peru invaded Ecuador. Peru claimed as its own most of the land in Equador's jungle region. Coffee plantations, gold mines, and oil reserves made the region valuable. Ecuador didn't want to give up these resources. Although in 1942 the two countries signed the Protocol of Peace, Friendship, and Boundaries giving the land to Peru, Ecuador soon claimed the land as its own again. Peru and Ecuador fought over the land for more than fifty years. In 1998, they finally reached agreements on border security and trade, access to the Amazon region and, most importantly, the location of the Peru-Ecuador border.

The economy improved after World War II, aided by an increased demand for Ecuador's bananas. The country's prosperity helped stabilize the government. President Galo Plaza Lasso, elected in 1948, was the first president to serve a complete term in over twenty years. Ecuador remained stable through the late 1950s.

The 1960s and 1970s brought growing unrest. Many poor people moved to the cities, trying to find work. Riots and strikes broke out when the government put new taxes into effect. A drop in banana exports aggravated the economic crisis. In the 1960s, governmental leadership changed often, with power passing from elected presidents to military leaders and back again. But through the 1970s, the military leaders were firmly in control.

During this same period, Ecuador started selling oil to other countries. The money from these sales was used to improve farming, transportation systems, and schools. Some people became very rich, but most Ecuadoreans remained poor. There was a growing demand to address the income differences among the population.

A dramatic drop in oil prices in the 1980s triggered another economic crisis in Ecuador. Because of its extensive borrowing in the 1970s, Ecuador owed nearly $7 billion (U.S. dollars) to foreign countries. Businesses were struggling, and prices for goods and services were rising quickly. These problems worsened when El Niño (L NEEN-yo), an unusual weather pattern, caused flooding and severe *drought* throughout the country.

In an effort to foster improvement, the people elected presidents who promised to make the country better by cutting spending and selling government-owned businesses to

opposite:
Ecuadorean president
Gustavo Naboa (left)
meets with South Korean
foreign minister Choi
Sung-hong on a trip to
Asia. The purpose of the
trip was to promote trade
and better relations
between Ecuador and
South Korea.

private companies. Some reforms were welcomed by the citizens, but there were widespread protests against others.

In 1996, Abdalá Bucaram (BOO-kah-rem) was elected president after promising to help the poor and fight corruption. Once he took office, though, he put economic policies in place that hurt the poor. In 1997, about 2 million people marched to protest against President Bucaram. They demanded that he be removed from office. Congress agreed and replaced Bucaram with Fabián Alarcón, the congressional leader.

Ecuador Today

Ecuador continued to struggle economically in the late 1990s. Heavy floods caused by El Niño weather patterns hurt farmers again. Ecuador's foreign debt was still increasing, and its money—the sucre—was not worth much. (The value of a country's money depends upon how much it can purchase. When a country prints extra money to pay for governmental operations, there is more money in circulation than there are goods to buy. Prices increase and the value of the money decreases. This is called *inflation*.)

Ecuador faced a catastrophic economic situation by 1999. The inflation rate was higher than in any other Latin American nation—over 100 percent. Banks were on the verge of collapse. The government stopped payments on its foreign debt.

In 2000, President Gustavo Noboa Bejarano changed Ecuador's money from the sucre (SOO-kreh) to the U.S. dollar. He changed laws so that other countries could invest in Ecuador's businesses. As a result of these changes, Ecuador received $2 billion in aid from the International Monetary Fund. This money strengthened Ecuador's banks.

With inflation under control and a balanced budget in place, Ecuador's economy has started to grow again. Not everyone is benefiting from the changes yet. More than half of the population is still classified as poor, earning less than $42 per month. Unemployment levels have reached as high as 40 percent. The government estimates that at least 400,000 Ecuadoreans left the country between 1998 and 2001. Their primary destinations were Spain and the United States.

From Sucres to Dollars

Each country has its own money system; coins and bills that are accepted as legal payment for goods and services. Some countries allow another country's currency—like the U.S. dollar—to be used in addition to their own. In recent years, some countries have considered replacing their own money with the U.S. dollar because its value doesn't change as often as their own. This usually results in a more stable economy. (The United States doesn't encourage other countries to use the U.S. dollar, but cannot stop a country from doing so.)

When the first proposal to switch Ecuador's sucre to the U.S. dollar was made in 2000, there were many protests. People in poor, rural areas were concerned that the change would make them even poorer. Some feared that Ecuador would lose part of its national identity by adopting the currency of another, stronger nation. Others looked forward to the change, anticipating a return to a more stable economy.

During a six-month transition period, both the sucre and the dollar were in circulation. As sucres were deposited in the banks, though, they were taken out of circulation. By September 2000, the U.S. dollar was the official currency of Ecuador. Inflation soon dropped.

Ecuadorean Population in the U.S.	
New York	136,100
New Jersey	72,038
Florida	40,525
Illinois	21,034
California	16,500

Source: U.S. Census, 2000

Coming to America

E cuador's history has been marked by turbulence. From the colonial era to the present, change–sometimes sudden, violent change–in the government has been a fact of life. These changes are often tied to times when the economy is very weak and many people are out of work.

When the United States adopted a more inclusive immigration policy in 1965, Ecuador was undergoing a period of economic problems and political instability. An increasing number of Ecuadoreans began seeking opportunities in other countries, including America. The number of Ecuadorean immigrants to the United States more than doubled from the 1960s to the 1990s.

U.S./Ecuadorean Immigration by Decade

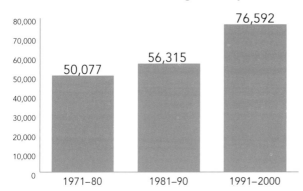

Source: Statistical Yearbook of the Immigration and Naturalization Service

In 2000, the U.S. Census counted about 350,000 people from Ecuador living in the United States. In recent years, most of the immigrants from Ecuador settled in the New York City area and Miami, Florida. Most of the immigrants from Ecuador enter the United States legally. But the Immigration and Naturalization Service estimates that 55,000 Ecuadoreans were living in the United States illegally as of 1996.

Sixto Durán Ballén, president of Ecuador from 1992 to 1996, did not have such a successful experience. His four years in office were marked by distrust and suspicion. Voters turned down Durán Ballén's proposed health care and government reforms after his vice-president fled the country to avoid charges of embezzlement.

Life in America

Like so many other immigrants, Ecuadoreans come to the United States searching for a better life. Because they come from a Spanish-speaking country, they are often seen as Hispanic or Latino rather than Ecuadorean or Ecuadorean American. On the positive side, this shared cultural background often makes adapting to life in a new country much easier. On the negative side, claiming the Hispanic or Latino label may feel like giving up one's own identity.

Family

Most Ecuadorean families settle in Spanish-speaking neighborhoods when they arrive in the United States. Ecuadorean families are very close. In Ecuador, grandparents, cousins, and in-laws often live in the same hometown or neighborhood. Extended families may share a home. This tradition of close ties makes the immigration process, with its often lengthy separation from family, a lonely time for many Ecuadorean immigrants.

In neighborhoods such as Jackson Heights in New York City, Spanish is used at bodegas, or markets, at church services, and in newspapers. Ecuadorean restaurants serve familiar foods. There are even branches of Ecuadorean banks and appliance stores to serve a growing Ecuadorean population. New immigrants adjusting to life in the United States find the familiar sounds and tastes very welcome. For most immigrants, sending for any family left behind in Ecuador is a top priority.

Work

The vast majority of Ecuadorean immigrants enter the United States through the family reunification program. Over half of those who reported their occupation in 2000 were professionals, managers, technical workers, sales representatives, or administrative support personnel. Nearly one-fifth find jobs in service areas, such as hotels, restaurants, and shops. Others work in factories and as laborers. Very few look for work in the farming or fishing industries due to their settlement in urban areas.

Two Spanish-speaking students work on an assignment in Yakima, Washington, as their bilingual teacher observes. School districts in communities like Yakima with large populations of Spanish-speaking immigrants have recently begun importing teachers from Latin countries to help students make the transition to American schools.

School

In America, children of Ecuadorean immigrants have many of the same experiences in school as other immigrant children. They often have to put up with teasing and name-calling because they look or speak differently from their classmates. Ecuador has a warm, almost tropical climate, and depending on where their family has settled, children may be unused to the weather and lack the right clothes to fit in with their class. They must learn a new language while they are trying to learn subjects such as science and math. Most urban schools offer extra help for students who are learning English. Many schools offer classes in English as a second language (ESL). Others have bilingual (BYE-ling-gwul) programs for Spanish-speaking students.

The Great Language Debate

Imagine that you start going to a new school. You don't understand what anyone is saying. You don't understand the questions that the teacher asks. And when you try to read something, none of the words make sense.

Students who don't speak or read English well often need extra help in school while they are learning their new language. The type of help they get depends upon where they are living and what language they speak.

Educators in some school districts, such as the one in Miami, Florida, believe that knowing more than one language is very important. They see that students who speak two or three languages have more job opportunities when they get older. These school districts usually offer *bilingual programs*. In these programs, students spend part of the school day learning English. They spend the rest of the day studying in their own language (Spanish, Haitian, or Chinese, for example). The people who believe bilingual education is best give these reasons why:

• Students can continue learning in subjects like science because they are taught in their own language.

• Students learn English quickly because they have support from teachers and students who share their language.

• Students end up knowing two languages instead of replacing their own language with English.

• Students who were born in the United States and speak English well can study another language in depth.

• People who know more than one language have more job opportunities and make more money than people who speak only one language.

Many other people believe that students should speak only English in school. People who believe that bilingual education doesn't work give these reasons:

• Students don't learn either language well when they are in bilingual programs.

• Students will not learn English quickly if they can use their own language to get information.

• The United States is an English-speaking country. Everyone who moves here should learn English right away.

Religion

The Spanish conquerors introduced the Roman Catholic religion to Ecuador. Today nearly everyone in Ecuador is Catholic. The Roman Catholic Church in America has always been a source of help to immigrants. When they come to America, their religious practices may be the one thing that doesn't require much change. In fact, as many as one-third of all Catholics in America are Hispanic.

The Catholic churches in neighborhoods with many immigrants usually conduct Mass in their native language. Many churches offer English classes. Some provide assistance in locating health care providers, food, and clothing. All of these services make it easier for new immigrants to adjust to life in the United States.

Holidays and Festivals

Immigrants to the United States continue to celebrate their traditional holidays. Sometimes the way the holiday is observed is slightly different than it would be if a family was back in their home country.

Since most Ecuadoreans are Roman Catholic, many of the holidays they celebrate are religious ones. These include Easter, All Soul's Day, and Christmas. Feasting, dancing, and parades mark many of the holidays in the cities and villages of Ecuador, and those celebrations are re-created in the United States.

One of the most popular festivals in Ecuador, Carnival, takes place before Lent, the forty-day period leading up to Easter. Like many Latin American countries, Ecuador celebrates Carnival for two or three days before Lent begins. Children and young people hide near the streets, waiting for people who are not paying attention to walk by. The children splash them with water, using water balloons, buckets, and anything else that will hold water as their tools. In America, these festivities last through the weekend and end on Monday when it's time to go back to work and school.

opposite:
Women dance in the streets
of Pujili, Ecuador, during
the Roman Catholic
Corpus Cristi celebration.

Along with many American Christians, Ecuadoreans spend the period of Lent preparing for Easter by reflecting on their spiritual life and repenting. During the week before Easter, Ecuadoreans take part in religious parades and processions, usually held in their local churches.

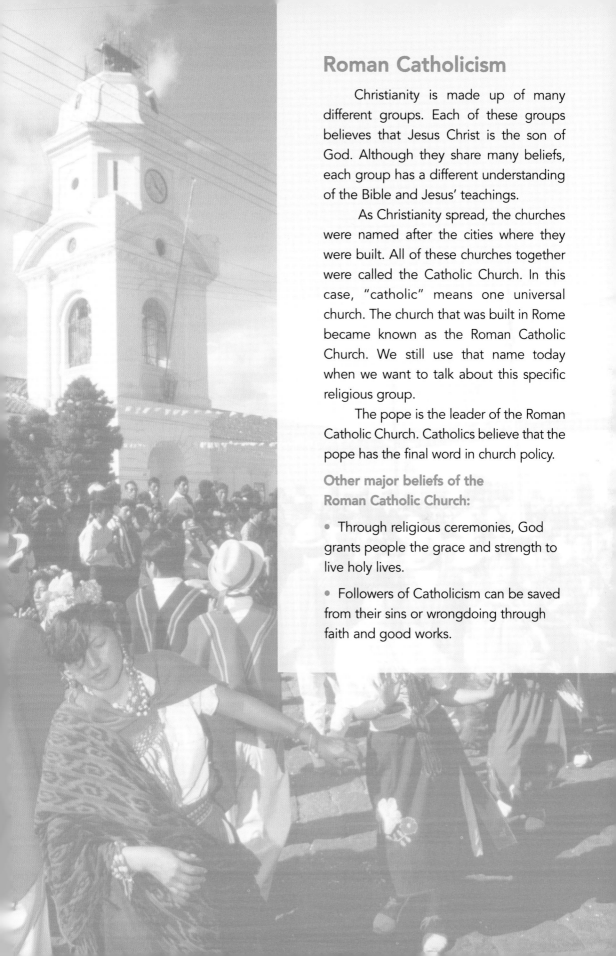

Roman Catholicism

Christianity is made up of many different groups. Each of these groups believes that Jesus Christ is the son of God. Although they share many beliefs, each group has a different understanding of the Bible and Jesus' teachings.

As Christianity spread, the churches were named after the cities where they were built. All of these churches together were called the Catholic Church. In this case, "catholic" means one universal church. The church that was built in Rome became known as the Roman Catholic Church. We still use that name today when we want to talk about this specific religious group.

The pope is the leader of the Roman Catholic Church. Catholics believe that the pope has the final word in church policy.

Other major beliefs of the Roman Catholic Church:

• Through religious ceremonies, God grants people the grace and strength to live holy lives.

• Followers of Catholicism can be saved from their sins or wrongdoing through faith and good works.

On All Soul's Day in November, families visit cemeteries to honor the dead, leaving flowers and offerings on the graves of friends and family members. If they are unable to return to their loved ones' graves, immigrants in America may go to church instead, lighting candles and saying prayers to honor the dead. They also dance and feast. This holiday gives people a chance to remember the happy times that they shared with those who have died.

A local flower merchant in Cuenca, Ecuador, studies her wares. Cuenca is one of the world's leading flower exporters. Located high in the Andes on the equator, the city has a mild climate year-round, ideal for growing flowering plants.

Ecuadorean immigrants can experience the same New Year's Eve parties and feasts in America that they once did in Ecuador. At midnight, people exchange kisses, just as in the United States. Then the party moves outside. In urban areas, Ecuadoreans hold block parties with celebration spilling onto the sidewalks and streets of a neighborhood. Each family makes a human figure, much like a scarecrow, to represent the year that is ending. In Ecuador, these figures are placed in the street and set on fire. Thus the old year is burned away to make room for the new. It is against the law to burn things in the street in most U.S. cities, so families usually hold their New Year's Eve feast without the ritual bonfire.

Food

Ecuadoreans in the United States can find most of the ingredients they need to make their traditional foods.

Ecuadoreans cook a lot of soups and stews. Rice and vegetables are a mainstay of the diet. *Aji* (AH-hee), hot sauce, is served at nearly every meal. Immigrants from different regions of Ecador have their own special dishes.

The coastal region offers dishes with a Spanish influence, featuring local seafood, coconut, peanuts, plantains, and bananas. Beans and lentils may be served with meals in place of potatoes. One of the most popular dishes along the coast is seviche. In this dish, fresh fish is cut up and covered with lemon or lime juice. The juice "cooks" the fish. The fish is then mixed with onions, hot peppers, and spices. In Ecuador, seviche is always served with popcorn. Food from the coastal region of Ecuador has risen in popularity in America.

The Sierra region covers the Andes Mountains. Most of the people living here are Amerindian. Potatoes, corn, and pork are often served in the Sierra. Two well-known specialties of this region are *locro de papas,* a potato stew, and *llapingachos,* potato cakes. *Cuy*—whole roasted guinea pig—is considered a special treat. These foods are commonly found in the United States, but Ecuadorean families may find themselves forgoing the hard work of preparing traditional meals in favor of the quicker, more convenient style of eating in America.

Bananas

If you've eaten many bananas in your life, chances are some came from Ecuador. Ecuador sells more bananas than any other country in the world. One out of every four bananas sold in the United States comes from Ecuador.

Locro de Papas
(Potato Soup)

Ecuadoreans often serve sliced avocados with locro.

4 tablespoons butter

1 teaspoon paprika

2 onions, finely chopped

4 cups water

4 pounds baking potatoes, peeled and diced

1 pound firm white fish (haddock, bass, or cod), cut into bite-sized pieces, optional

2 cups half-and-half

2 eggs, lightly beaten

1 cup grated Muenster cheese

Salt and pepper to taste

Melt the butter in a large saucepan and add the paprika. Add the onions and sauté until they are soft. Add the water and bring it to a boil. Add the potatoes. Simmer uncovered over low heat, stirring occasionally, until the potatoes are almost done. (If necessary, add more water during cooking.)

Add the fish (if desired) and the half-and-half. Continue cooking, stirring occasionally, until the potatoes begin to fall apart.

Stir a little of the potato mixture into the beaten eggs, then add the eggs to the soup. Remove from the heat, stir in the cheese, and season with the salt and pepper. Serve immediately.

Serves 6.

Source: Adapted from South American Cooking: Foods & Feasts from the New World *by Barbara Karoff*

CHAPTER TWO

Ethiopians

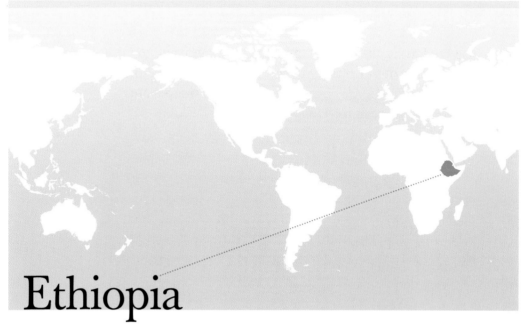

Ethiopia

has a rich history of independence. Except for five years of occupation by Italy (1936–1941), Ethiopia has never been ruled by another country. It is the oldest independent nation in Africa and one of the oldest in the world.

The people of Ethiopia are divided into four main groups: Amhara, Tigray, Oromo, and Somali. Most Amhara and Tigray people live in the northern highlands and are Ethiopian Orthodox Christians. They share a common heritage as well: their *ancestors* ruled the ancient kingdom of Aksum. The Amharic language, once the official language of the Ethiopian empire, is still arguably the most important. It is widely used in business and government, and about half of the population speaks Amharic as either a native or second language.

The Oromo are probably the largest group within Ethiopia. Over the centuries they have expanded from their homeland in south-central Ethiopia into several different regions. As a result, there are several different groups within the Oromo people. Some are farmers; others live in urban areas. Some practice traditional religions; others are Ethiopian Orthodox Christian, Protestant, or Muslim.

In the southern lowlands are the Somali, a group that is related to the people in neighboring Somalia. They are predominantly Muslim, with a history of conflict and resistance against the Ethiopian government.

A Quick Look Back

Legend has it that the great King Solomon and the beautiful, mysterious Queen of Sheba had a son named Menelik, who built the empire of Ethiopia and whose *descendants* ruled it for many years.

Ancient Times

The ancient kingdom of Aksum was the first of the Ethiopian empires. It covered most of the northern regions, home to the Amhara and Tigray people today. The royal family claimed to be related to King Solomon and so became known as the Solomonid *dynasty*. Located on the eastern coast of Africa, Aksum controlled many trade routes, including the Red Sea.

As traders, the Aksumites met and worked with people of many different nations and religions, including Jews and, in the first century A.D., Christians. By the beginning of the fourth century, Aksum's emperor, Ezana, converted to Christianity. It became the official religion of the empire and most Aksumites became Christians. For many centuries, Aksum was a large, powerful country.

From the seventh to the ninth centuries, Islam spread from the nearby Arabian Peninsula to the coastal and southern regions of Aksum. By the tenth century, the Aksum kingdom had lost much of its power. Another powerful family, the Zagwé dynasty, ruled for over 300 years before the Solomonids took control again.

How much salt for those shoes?

Aksum was the only ancient African empire to produce coins. Only the royal family and nobles used these coins, inlaid with gold and bronze or silver. Everyone else used salt or iron bars for money.

Continued Independence

Throughout the sixteenth and seventeenth centuries, Ethiopia's emperors struggled to retain the country's independence. They fought off Islamic invaders as well as missionaries who tried to convert Ethiopian Orthodox Christians to Roman Catholicism. Ethiopia's success led to a general belief that the Ethiopian Church was central to Ethiopian's independence. Although the period was marked by confusion and conflict, there was also a new focus on artistic expression, especially architecture.

During the late 1800s, Ethiopia fought off many invasions by Egypt. It was also attacked by Sudan. But the biggest threat came from Italy after the Suez Canal opened in 1869, providing a shortcut from Europe and America to southern Asia and eastern Africa. By 1885, Italy had established a *colony* in Eritrea, on the coast of the Red Sea. The two countries signed a *treaty,* but because they interpreted the agreement differently, a war broke out. Italian forces moved south into Ethiopia in 1895. The Ethiopians were determined to remain independent. After a year of fighting, they forced Italy to retreat. Ethiopia remained an independent nation, in charge of its own affairs.

The Last Ethiopian Emperor

Emperor Haile Selassie (HI-lee SAH-lass-ee) came to power in Ethiopia in 1930. His move to modernize Ethiopia's government was interrupted by a second invasion by Italy in 1935. This time, Italian troops were successful in capturing Ethiopia.

It wasn't until Italy joined forces with Hitler in 1940 that any other country stepped in to help Ethiopia. British troops helped Ethiopian resistance fighters defeat the Italians, and Haile Selassie returned to the throne in 1941.

Selassie's government made changes to improve life in Ethiopia. The most important change gave everyone the right to vote, although educated and wealthy people were the most likely to exercise this right. The United States and Ethiopia developed strong ties during this time.

After Italy and Germany were defeated and World War II ended, the United Nations (UN) decided to make Ethiopia and Eritrea (EH-ri-tree-ah, a former Italian colony) partners in a federation. Each country would have its own government; Ethiopia would manage foreign affairs. After the decision was made, Ethiopia took control of Eritrea anyway. This action gave Ethiopia free access to the Red Sea once more, expanding its base for commerce. But it also prompted a group of Eritrean rebels to fight for their freedom.

The 1960s was a turbulent time for Ethiopia. An attempted coup failed to force Selassie from office. Fighting along the Somalian border caused many problems. There was also trouble with Sudan, which supported the Eritrean freedom fighters. Economic problems began to surface.

Emperor Haile Selassie reviews his troops in this 1965 photograph.

A long period without rain in the early 1970s caused many crops to fail. People didn't have enough to eat and many starved to death. Jobs were hard to find. Selassie was blamed for many of these problems. In 1974, he was overthrown by an organization of military officers called the Derg (derj). The Derg declared that Ethiopia would become a *socialist* republic, a form of government in which the economy is controlled by the state.

The Red Terror

By 1977, Major Haile Mariam Mengistu, a member of the Derg, had established himself as a dictator. The Ethiopian People's Revolutionary Party (EPRP) challenged Mengistu's leadership and killed many of his supporters, including members of the Derg, in an attack called the White Terror. Mengistu responded with the Red Terror. He gave weapons to people who supported his government and told them to find any neighbors who were enemies of the state. In the late 1970s, the Red Terror campaign resulted in about 100,000 people being killed or disappearing. Thousands left Ethiopia for refugee camps in other countries.

In protest against Mengistu's actions, the United States refused to give Ethiopia any further military help. Rebel groups quickly took advantage of this situation. They reclaimed several regions in Ethiopia from Mengistu. Overwhelmed, Mengistu asked the Soviet Union for help. Eager to gain influence and extend the reach of Communism, the Soviet Union and Cuba sent troops to help Mengistu regain control of Ethiopia.

Refugee camps and emergency feeding centers such as this one in the Danakil Desert in Bati were set up by international agencies to help Ethiopia's starving population. Despite these efforts, many people died each day of starvation and related diseases as a result of the famines in the 1970s and 1980s.

Starvation and Rebellion

Long periods without rain in the late 1970s and mid-1980s created severe food shortages and famine in northern Ethiopia. Organizations around the world sent food and supplies, but Mengistu often let the food rot in the warehouses instead of providing it to people who might oppose him. By keeping people dependent upon him, Mengistu kept his power, but in the process about a million Ethiopians died of starvation during the 1980s.

The Eritrean and Tigray rebels took over key regions and cities in 1987. Mengistu's army needed more troops to fight against the rebels. He ordered his soldiers to kidnap men and boys and force them to serve in the army. Many families with young boys left Ethiopia or sent their sons to another country so they wouldn't have to fight for Mengistu.

Mengistu's government was in trouble. He held peace talks with the rebel leaders. But when rebel forces took control of Eritrea in 1991 and surrounded Addis Ababa, the capital city of Ethiopia, Mengistu gave up and left the country.

In 1993, Eritrea declared itself to be an independent country once more and was recognized as separate by the new Ethiopian government. Ethiopia's interim leader, Meles Zenawi (MEL-ez ZEN-ah-wee), and a group of elected representatives gathered in 1994 to write a new *constitution* and elect new representatives. The country was renamed the Federal Democratic Republic of Ethiopia.

Ethiopia Today

An argument over the location of the Ethiopian-Eritrean border set off fighting in 1998. With both sides sending thousands of troops to the border, a war broke out. The two countries finally signed a peace treaty in December 2000.

Although Ethiopia is still adjusting after decades of *civil war,* the economy was starting to grow again in 1999–2000. However, low coffee prices and continuing *drought* devastated many areas of the country in 2002. Coffee farmers, most of whom replaced their food crops with coffee trees, now have nothing to eat and no money with which to buy food. At the end of 2002, humanitarian organizations were organizing to help over 6 million Ethiopians affected by the drought.

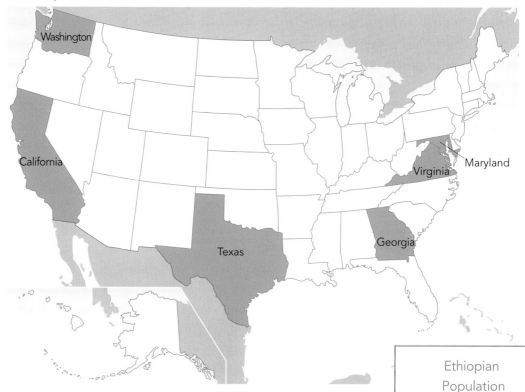

Ethiopian Population in the U.S.	
California	10,232
Texas	9,736
Virginia	8,803
Georgia	8,238
Maryland	7,387
Washington	6,477

Source: U.S. Census, 2000

Coming to America

E thiopians have traveled to the United States for many years, both for business and for education. Until recently, few chose to settle in the United States. This was due in part to limits on the number of *immigrants* from African countries. Another reason was the cost of immigrating; most Ethiopians could not afford to travel around the world. Another reason was America's history of slavery and racism. Many Africans didn't want to immigrate until conditions improved.

For most Ethiopians, making a decision to leave their homeland permanently is a difficult one. When the dictator Mengistu took control of the country in the mid-1970s, he killed many people. Refugees fled the violence in Ethiopia in large numbers.

U.S./Ethiopian Immigration by Decade

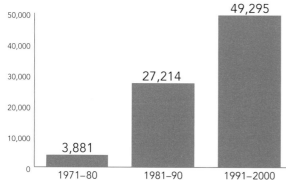

Source: Statistical Yearbook of the Immigration and Naturalization Service

The long drought and terrible food shortages in the 1980s forced even more people to leave. About half of the Ethiopians who arrived in America during the 1980s were refugees.

Another wave of immigrants and refugees arrived in the early 1990s when rebel forces gained control of the country. A third wave arrived at the end of the century when war broke out between Ethiopia and Eritrea. Many of these refugees *resettled* in the United States.

Although a large number of refugees arrived during the 1990s, they were outnumbered by immigrants. Some immigrants entered through the employment preference program. Others rejoined family members who had immigrated earlier.

Most of the immigrants from Ethiopia settle in cities. The Washington, D.C., area has one of the largest Ethiopian communities in the nation. Other top destinations for Ethiopian immigrants are Texas, California, Georgia, and Washington State.

Although the United States is very far away from Africa, both in distance and in cultural tradition, most Ethiopians feel the move has been worthwhile. There are many opportunities here and, with hard work, they can make a better life.

Spotlight on
SELAMAWI (MAWI) HAILEAB ASEGDOM

"What's both beautiful and scary about young children is that they will believe most anything that their parents tell them. If our parents had told us that black refugees growing up on welfare in an affluent white community couldn't excel, we probably would have believed them. But they told us that we could do anything if we worked hard and treated others with respect. And we believed them."

—Mawi Asegdom

Selamawi (Mawi) Haileab Asegdom and his family undertook a journey that most Americans cannot imagine. They left their beloved but war-torn Ethiopia for a refugee camp in Sudan, a country sharing Ethiopia's western border. Later, they left Africa to start a new life in the United States. Mawi's experiences as he grew from a child to a young man, from a refugee to the commencement speaker at Harvard, are described in his book *Of Beetles and Angels*.

Mawi was seven years old when he and his siblings left Ethiopia with their mother. They walked hundreds of miles to reach Sudan. His father had left earlier when it had become clear that he was going to be arrested or worse for providing medical care to anyone who needed it.

The family was reunited in the refugee camp. They had not planned to continue on to the United States. But Mawi's mother and father decided that America would provide their children with the best opportunities. Three years after arriving in Sudan, the Asegdom family was on its way to a suburb of Chicago, Illinois.

Despite homesickness and family tragedy, Mawi was determined to excel in school. He succeeded beyond even his own expectations. He won a full scholarship to Harvard. And at the end of his college career, he was chosen by his classmates to give the graduation speech. Today Mawi is an author and motivational speaker.

Life in America

Ethiopians who immigrate to the United States are often faced with culture shock. The nonstop pace of American life, the influence of television, and differences in everything from food to holidays can give new immigrants a sense of isolation. Although the United States offers many opportunities, it also threatens their sense of self–their cultural identity.

These problems are often made worse by the racism that African immigrants encounter. They expect that some white Americans will judge them by the color of their skin. It is often a surprise, though, to find that they are not always welcome among African Americans in their communities.

Although many Ethiopians plan to live in the United States permanently, becoming a citizen is a step that some are not ready to take. For some Ethiopians, becoming an American citizen means that they have given up hope of returning to their homeland. Others wait to become citizens for a more practical reason: American citizens have to give up their family inheritances in Ethiopia.

Family

Ethiopian families want their children to take advantage of the opportunities that America offers. At the same time, they are concerned that children won't lose touch with Ethiopian traditions of respect for elders and authority.

In areas in the United States with large Ethiopian communities, cultural associations and culture schools introduce young people to the traditions and language of their homeland. The programs at these schools help students learn or maintain their native language so they can talk with relatives when they visit Ethiopia. They teach Ethiopian manners, such as speaking softly. They also give young people a clear understanding of who they are and how they fit into the world.

People who work with immigrants and refugees know that programs like these help parents keep their families together as they learn to fit into American society. Children are less likely to be affected by negative influences in their school or neighborhood, like gangs and drugs, if they maintain ties to their heritage.

Aster Begne was a political prisoner in Ethiopia for eight months before escaping to America, where she joined her husband and children.

Work

The work opportunities for Ethiopians in the United States depend in large part upon the path they take to get here. Immigrants who are granted visas through the employment preference program or through the *diversity lottery* come to the United States with a strong educational background. They may already know English. They generally do not have problems finding work. Refugees may or may not be educated. Those who are may have experience that doesn't apply to jobs here. If they do not speak English, they are likely to be stuck in a low-paying job.

As the Ethiopian community in America grows, more immigrants open their own businesses, ranging from restaurants and grocery stores to dress shops and services. Most of these businesses have a large base of immigrant customers. The money to start these businesses may come from a savings club. Each member of the club puts a certain amount of money into the club each week or month. Then they take turns receiving the money that has built up. In this way, immigrants who may not qualify for a loan from a bank can save enough money to start a business.

School

Going to school in a new place is always difficult at first. It is especially difficult when you don't understand the language or customs. Unlike in America, there is no one official language in Ethiopia although Amharic is probably the most widespread of the traditional languages. Refugees in particular may find themselves in areas where there are few other Ethiopian immigrants and where English as a second language programs may not be offered.

Ethiopian students have also had to put up with name-calling and teasing, both from white and from African American classmates who consider them too foreign.

Students sometimes feel they have little in common with their American classmates, especially when they enter the United States as refugees. One boy who walked over 250 miles (400 kilometers) to reach safety in a refugee camp had trouble understanding his classmates' complaints about walking a few blocks to school.

Religion

When Ethiopians arrive in America, they are relieved to know they can practice whatever religion they choose. Many religious groups are found in Ethiopia. Although Christians were in the majority throughout much of Ethiopia's history, today there are more Muslims. Most of the Muslims live in the southeastern region of Ethiopia. Jewish people have a long history in Ethiopia as well. But, after centuries of discrimination and poverty, most have moved to Israel. Any Jews who do come to America find support and a place to worship at local synagogues.

Ethiopian Orthodox Christians

The church plays an important role in many people's lives in the United States. Church services in the native language and opportunities for fellowship with people from their country help Ethiopian immigrants adjust to life in the United States. Many churches sponsor language and culture schools that encourage children to learn about their heritage.

One of Ethiopia's oldest religions is the Ethiopian Orthodox Church. Orthodox churches hold beliefs that are similar to those of Roman Catholicism, but the Ethiopian Orthodox Church is unique even in the Orthodox community. With the introduction of Islam in Africa, Ethiopians were isolated from other Orthodox Christians for 500 years. They developed their own customs, placing more emphasis on the Old Testament than other Christian churches do. Fasting is an important part of Ethiopian Orthodoxy. The devout believers observe 250 fasting days each year, while "good" Christians fast 180 days. Fasts are broken at sundown, but only vegetarian meals can be eaten on those days.

Islam

One of the first mentions of Muslims in Ethiopia was in the early seventh century. The Prophet Mohammad's wife and cousins sought refuge in Aksum from persecution in Mecca. Refer to *The Newest Americans A–D*, pages 33–34 for more information about Islam.

Religions of Ethiopia

a Muslim 45%
b Ethiopian Orthodox 40%
c Other 15%

Source: CIA World Factbook, 2002

Holidays and Festivals

Ethiopians celebrate some of the same holidays that Americans do, but at a different time. This happens because Ethiopia uses the calendar and teachings of the Ethiopian Orthodox Church to determine holidays. This calendar has thirteen months instead of twelve. There are thirty days in the first twelve months. The thirteenth month has five or six days, depending upon whether it is leap year. The years are also different; 2003 is considered to be 1996 in Ethiopia.

Orthodox Christians celebrate Christmas on January 7. They celebrate Easter later than other Christians do, although the exact date varies from year to year. Meskal is another Orthodox holiday. It honors the legend of the Empress Helena's finding the "true cross," the cross on which Jesus was crucified, in A.D. 326. Bonfires are part of the traditional celebration in Ethiopia. In Washington, D.C., the Ethiopian American community celebrates Meskal with an outdoor candlelight ceremony.

A young Ethiopian immigrant decorates a gingerbread house during a holiday festival in her new home of Kodiak, Alaska.

Ethiopian New Year

The Ethiopian New Year (Inqutatash) occurs in September, after months of heavy rain come to an end. It is harvest season—a good time to say good-bye to the old year and welcome the new. Like people everywhere, Ethiopians think about their hopes for the future as the New Year begins.

In America, people begin getting ready for Inqutatash days in advance. They buy food for their New Year's feast along with candles and torches, to simulate the dried leaves and wood they would burn in Ethiopia on the evening before Inqutatash.

The New Year begins with singing as young girls walk around the neighborhood, serenading each home. Boys also visit the homes in their neighborhoods, offering drawings as gifts. People give the children small gifts or coins to thank them for their songs and drawings. In America, members of an Ethiopian community might gather in a church or meeting place to celebrate these traditions.

For some immigrants, the fun of their New Year's celebration is echoed in the American holiday of Halloween.

The Arts

Music and dance offer many Ethiopian immigrants the chance to celebrate their culture and to share it with others. Music is a vital part of Ethiopian tradition, performed in church services, at community events, and in homes.

The Nile Ethiopian Ensemble was the first group to perform the folk music and dances in the United States. Many of the performers learned to dance or play their instruments as children in Ethiopia. Today they perform dances from several different ethnic groups. Their performances help Americans better understand what it is to be Ethiopian.

Ethiopian immigrants have adopted music from other cultures as well. One of the most popular types of music is reggae. Reggae music started in Jamaica. In reggae songs, Ethiopia often stands for African heritage. Reggae is extremely popular with young Americans; this similarity in musical taste makes Ethiopian students feel less isolated.

A Dorze woman cooks injera, *a part of the national Ethiopian dish,* injera *and* wat.

Food

Immigrant families make an effort to gather everyone for meals in the United States just as they do in their home country. This is often difficult, though. Both parents may have to work long hours to support the family. Children may be involved in after-school activities in the late afternoon or early evening. Parents maintain, however, that eating together is an important tradition to uphold. It is a time when family members can share what is happening in their lives. Children also learn about their culture in an informal way as they hear proverbs or stories about the past.

Even if families have trouble making time for a traditional meal, they try to serve Ethiopian foods regularly. This is easy for today's immigrants. Grocery stores that serve areas with large Ethiopian communities often carry the ingredients needed for traditional foods. Ethiopian restaurants offer families in several cities another way to introduce traditional foods to their children and friends.

Traditional foods are not just a part of daily life for many immigrants. They are also part of every celebration, including those that mark births, marriages, and deaths. Some Ethiopian immigrants have started their own businesses by cooking traditional foods for parties and celebrations. Ethiopian foods are made with many different spices, a reminder of the trade routes that passed through the country from its earliest years. Spices such as ginger and chili peppers were introduced from Portugal and Asia. These combine with other Ethiopian spices to create some very hot and spicy dishes.

Wat, or stew, is the traditional dish of Ethiopia. It may be made with chicken, beef, or as a vegetarian dish. It is always spicy, whether it is made with meat or not.

Traditional meals are served with *injera,* a flat, round, spongy bread that looks like a pancake. At meals, the *wat* or other main dish is spooned onto an *injera* at the center of the table. More *injera* are used in place of forks and spoons. To eat the meal, one tears off a piece of *injera* and uses it to grab some of the *wat.* When the *wat* is finished, the *injera* in the center of the table can be eaten.

The Ethiopian Coffee Ceremony

Many people in the United States start their day with a cup of coffee or drink coffee during the day. Most people drink their coffee without even thinking about it.

In Ethiopia, the birthplace of coffee, the traditional coffee ceremony offers much more than a break from routine. It is a time when family and friends gather to enjoy the ancient custom and each other's company.

The ceremony begins when the mother of an Ethiopian family invites people for *buna,* or coffee. She spreads a small mat on the floor. Grass and flowers are scattered over the mat to show humans' connection with nature. Then she places a wooden tray on the mat. The tray holds small porcelain coffee cups with no handles.

Green coffee beans are roasted over a burner until they are a rich brown. Everyone enjoys the smell of the roasted beans. The beans are then crushed and added to boiling water. Sometimes cinnamon or another spice is added to the mix. After the coffee has boiled, the grounds must settle.

When the coffee is ready, the mother holds the coffeepot above the tray and pours the coffee into the small cups. They are passed to the people at the ceremony, along with popcorn or bread. The pouring is repeated two more times. The ceremony may take one to two hours. During this time, friends often share stories with one another.

Ethiopians eat a large number of vegetarian dishes, due in large part to the number of fasting days observed by Ethiopian Orthodox Christians. On these days, nothing can be eaten or drunk between dawn and dusk. Meals to break the fast cannot include any animal products, including chicken, meat, fish, eggs, or dairy products. Lentils and other legumes are used quite often in vegetarian dishes.

Since the Kaffia region of Ethiopia is considered to be the birthplace of coffee, coffee is very important. It is offered after traditional meals. It is also served during the traditional coffee ceremony.

Shiro Wat (Lentil Stew)

Ethiopian Orthodox Christians rely on vegetarian dishes such as this one to break their many fasts.

2 cups dried lentils (1 pound), rinsed and picked over

2 tablespoons vegetable oil

1 yellow onion, finely chopped

2 garlic cloves, minced

1 or 2 small fresh red chilies

1 teaspoon salt

Ground black pepper

Place the lentils in a heavy saucepan and add enough water to cover by 2 inches. Bring to a boil, then reduce the heat to medium-low and simmer until tender, 30 to 45 minutes. Mash with a fork.

In a skillet over medium heat, warm the oil. Add the onion, garlic, and chilies. Sauté until soft, about 5 minutes. Add the mashed lentils, salt, and pepper to taste. Cook until the flavors are blended and the mixture is heated through, 8 to 10 minutes. Taste for seasoning and serve.

Makes 6 to 8 servings.

Source: Soul and Spice: African Cooking in the Americas *by Heidi Haughy Cusick*

CHAPTER THREE

Filipinos

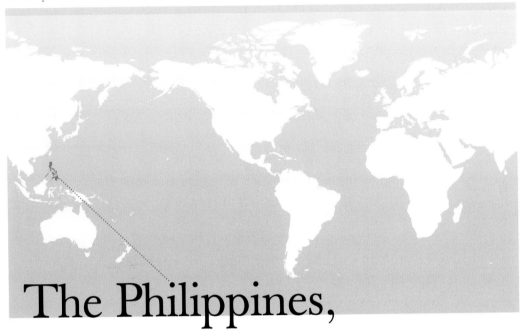

The Philippines,

a group of over 7,000 islands in the western Pacific Ocean, lie just off the coast of China. The people who live here come from many cultures. The Malay people, *ancestors* to the majority of Filipinos, traveled from Malaysia to settle on the islands. Traders from China and India followed. They were joined by Spanish *conquerors* and American colonists.

The Philippines are divided into three main regions. Languages and cultures are different within these regions. But English and Philipino are the official languages throughout the islands. The major island–Luzon–is the largest island in the Philippines. It is home to the capital city of Manila. The region south of Luzon is called the Visayan (VI-say-en) Islands. The third region includes Mindanao and the Sulu Islands at the southernmost tip of the Philippines. Most of the people living in this area are Muslim.

The Philippine Islands were a colony of the United States for nearly fifty years, from 1898 to 1946. Filipinos have traveled to the United States in search of the American Dream ever since.

A Quick Look Back

Not much is known about the earliest settlers in the Philippine Islands. They probably arrived during the Ice Age, traveling over ancient land bridges connecting Southeast Asia to Malaysia, Indonesia, and the Philippines. Around the third century B.C., the Malay people began to settle the islands. Early communities were family-based and women were highly respected. These early people traded goods with other Asian countries. As more traders visited the islands, new customs and religions were introduced, including Islam in the fourteenth century.

Spanish Colony

Ferdinand Magellan, the Spanish explorer, was the first European to reach the Philippines. A few decades later, in 1542, Spain claimed the islands and named them after Prince Philip. Spain wanted to use the Philippines as its trading base in Asia. Over the next three and a half centuries, Spain controlled the islands. It converted most of the islanders to Christianity, but Muslims on the southern island of Mindanao and on the Sulu Islands were not won over so easily. They fought against Spanish rule for over 300 years.

The Spanish colony quickly became divided by race and wealth. Spanish colonists and their children formed the upper class. Chinese *immigrants* were welcomed to islands where they soon became wealthy merchants and landowners. The native people were called indios. Most were farmworkers, although there was a growing middle class.

In the 1800s, Filipinos began calling for more representation in their government, but Spain refused to make any changes. In 1872, the execution of three Filipino priests and the *exile* of several reform leaders, including Dr. José Rizal (REE-sal), angered Filipinos. A secret group that wanted to overthrow the Spanish government formed. When the Spanish government found out about the group in 1896, they brought Rizal back from exile and executed him. The Spanish officials thought that killing Rizal would crush the Filipinos' spirit. Instead, the rebellion quickly spread through the whole country. A year of fighting ended in a truce in 1897. Spain agreed to institute land and governmental reforms within three years.

Dr. José Rizal

Dr. José Rizal was a fifth-generation Chinese mestizo from a well-to-do family. He was an ophthalmic surgeon, poet, and novelist. He was also one of the leaders of the reform movement in the mid-1800s. His execution sparked a violent revolt against the Spanish government. Today José Rizal is considered one of the national heroes of the Philippines.

The Spanish-American War broke out in Cuba in early 1898 and soon spread to the Philippines. American naval leaders urged the rebel troops to fight against Spain. The Filipinos took this as a sign that the United States supported their bid for independence, especially since their *constitution* was based on the U.S. Constitution. During the peace *treaty* process later that year, however, the Filipinos were left out of the negotiations. Spain gave control of the Philippines to the United States and received $20 million from the United States in return.

U.S. Territory and Commonwealth

Filipinos refused to accept their new status as an American colony, and the Philippine-American War broke out in 1899. After two years of fighting, over 20,000 soldiers were dead, most of them Filipino. Thousands of civilians died as well.

Once the war ended in 1901, the United States ruled fairly peacefully. Its intent was to set up a democratic government so Filipinos could rule themselves. As a start, many elected government positions were open to Filipinos. The United States also set up a national school system. Teachers from America taught the basics, including English, to millions of Filipino children. They also shared the promise of the American dream—that in the United States anything was possible through hard work. This dream inspired many Filipinos to immigrate to the United States.

However, the development of trade relations between the Philippines and the United States affected many Filipinos negatively. Wealthy landowners provided seed and cash advances to peasants who planted and harvested crops in return for a share of the profits. The interest on the loans grew quickly and the peasants soon owed more money than they could ever repay. Children became responsible for their parents' debt and before long, entire families were virtually slaves. Resistance movements began to form in the mid-1920s to combat the inequality.

The Philippines became a commonwealth in 1934 when the United States promised independence within ten years. Filipinos now controlled their national government, but any decisions on foreign trade and immigration had to be approved by the United States.

Attacks by the Japanese on Hawaii and the Philippines drew the United States into World War II in 1941. By 1942, the American and Filipino forces on the islands were forced to surrender to the Japanese. The prisoners were forced to march without food or water for hundreds of miles to the prisoner-of-war camps on Bataan peninsula. Thousands died on the Bataan death march, from starvation, disease, and torture.

Some Filipino government officials and wealthy landowners were later accused of collaborating with the Japanese during their occupation of the Philippines. The peasant farmers, on the other hand, were treated harshly by the Japanese. As a result, they formed *guerrilla* groups such as the Huks to fight against the Japanese.

Republic of the Philippines

Philippine independence was postponed for a few years because of World War II. But on July 4, 1946, Filipinos took complete control of their country. The United States retained the right to keep military bases on the Philippines. On the economic front, there was still a big gap between the wealthy landowners and the poor who worked on their land. The Huks and other guerrilla groups began attacking the government, hoping to introduce *Communism* to the Philippines.

After serving as secretary of defense and helping to crush the guerrilla movement, Ramón Magsaysay was elected president in 1953. He was very popular and his government worked toward reform. One of his most controversial plans was to purchase land on the southern island of Mindanao. The poor, mostly Catholic, families from other islands were given the opportunity to *resettle* there. The Muslims who had been in control of Mindanao for centuries resented being outnumbered by Christians. They eventually established the Moro National Liberation Front and began fighting to secede from the Philippines in the 1970s.

The Marcos Years

Ferdinand Marcos ruled the Philippines from 1965 to 1986. Faced with a slowing economy and attacks by guerrilla forces, Marcos declared martial law in 1972. This meant that the army, led by Marcos, would enforce the laws. Political opponents were arrested. Newspapers could print only the stories that Marcos approved. Many of the best-educated Filipinos immigrated to other countries during the Marcos regime, seeking an escape from his dictatorship.

Marcos allowed elections to be held again in 1981. He was elected to another six-year term because his opponents refused to run for office or vote, saying that the elections wouldn't be fair.

Benigno Aquino (BEN-neen-oh AH-keen-oh) was a popular leader of one of the groups that opposed Marcos. When he returned from exile in 1983, Aquino was assassinated. Suddenly, newspapers around the world started paying attention to what was happening in the Philippines. The people who opposed Marcos grew stronger in their demands for change.

A Change in Government

To quiet the protesters, Marcos called for a "snap" election in 1986. Because the election wasn't scheduled, Marcos thought he would have an advantage. Corazon Aquino, the widow of the man who had been killed, ran against Marcos.

Both sides said they had won the election. A four-day protest known as the People Power Movement led Marcos to flee the country. He left the country billions of dollars in debt and in a deep recession.

Corazon Aquino's first actions as president were to free political prisoners, restore freedom of the press, and get rid of corrupt officials. Her government struggled with issues of land reform and the demands for Muslim independence. During her term, the United States gave in to local demands and closed its military bases on the Philippines.

Former president Corazon Aquino's election signaled the end of the Marcos era and the return of democracy in the Philippines.

The Philippines Today

During the 1990s, democratic reform was a top priority. The *economy* began to grow in the early 1990s but suffered from the recession that hit Asia in 1997. Unemployment remains a serious problem.

The Moro Islamic Liberation Front (MILF), a Muslim group, continued to demand a separate Islamic nation in Mindanao. The ongoing fighting has killed at least 120,000 people over the past thirty years. President Gloria Macapagal-Arroyo signed a cease-fire agreement with the MILF in 2001. The Filipino military continues to fight terrorist groups in the area, however.

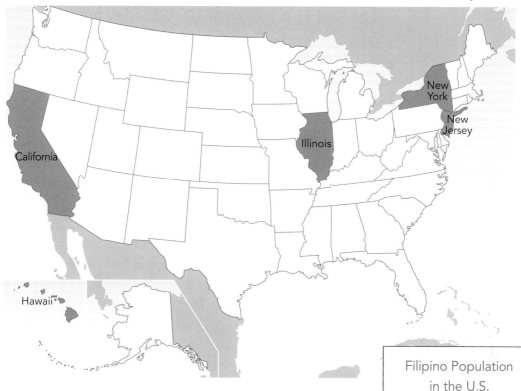

Filipino Population in the U.S.	
California	910,651
Hawaii	165,657
New Jersey	107,265
Illinois	94,488
New York	75,942

Source: U.S. Census, 2000

Coming to America

Filipinos began immigrating to the United States about 100 years ago. Today they are the largest group of Asian immigrants. Overall, only Mexico sends more people to the United States each year. Nevertheless, Filipinos are often called the invisible or forgotten immigrants, because so many have blended into their communities. Many of the immigrants are well-educated and have achieved a comfortable life in the United States. Most speak English fluently. They are often mistaken for Hispanics since many have a Spanish name and are Roman Catholics.

About 2.1 million Filipinos lived in the United States in 2000. Over three-fourths were born in the Philippines. Most of the immigrants have become U.S. citizens.

There are also some Filipinos living in the United States illegally. They generally come to the United

U.S./Filipino Immigration by Decade

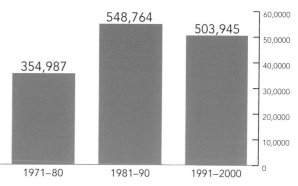

1971–80	1981–90	1991–2000
354,987	548,764	503,945

Source: Statistical Yearbook of the Immigration and Naturalization Service

States legally—on a tourist visa, as a temporary worker, or as a student. But when they are supposed to return home, some don't. In 1996, the Immigration and Naturalization Service estimated that about 95,000 Filipinos were living in the United States illegally.

Early Immigration

The first big wave of immigrants came to the United States in the early 1900s. As citizens of an American colony, Filipinos were allowed to move freely back and forth between the islands and the United States. Most went to nearby Hawaii, where they worked in the sugarcane fields. Within a few years, Filipinos began immigrating to the West Coast states as well. They worked in agriculture in California, Oregon, and Washington as well as in Alaskan fish canneries.

Nearly all of the immigrants expected to return home within a few years. Their dream was to make enough money to buy land in the Philippines and provide for their families. Work in the fields was difficult, though. Hours were long and pay was low. It was difficult to make enough money to support their families in the Philippines and to save for the future. As Filipino immigrants made a life for themselves in America, many made the decision to stay.

This Filipino immigrant was one of many who worked as farm laborers in California during the first half of the twentieth century.

Not all of the first immigrants were farmworkers. Some Filipinos traveled to the mainland United States to go to college. The U.S. government paid for some students' education. In return, these students agreed to work for the Philippine government after graduating. Other students worked part-time in service jobs in restaurants or hotels or as domestic servants to pay for their schooling. The students who chose to remain in the United States after they received their degree often had problems finding employment in their field due to the pervasive anti-Asian sentiment in America at the time. Many Filipinos with professional degrees could only find work as janitors.

Those who attended school in the United States were a source of pride. Their success, both in the United States and upon their return home, made others dream of immigrating to America.

America's Great Depression in the early 1930s left many Americans without work. With all their attention focused on their own economic survival, many Americans had little compassion for immigrants. As in other periods of economic hardship, *nativists* blamed immigrants for their inability to find a job. Given the large numbers of Filipinos in the United States, they were an easy target for Americans' frustration and blame. Discrimination and violence against Filipino workers grew. States began passing laws preventing Filipinos from marrying white people.

New federal laws were enacted during this time as well. The Tydings-McDuffie Act of 1934 promised full independence to the Philippines in 1944. Although Filipinos eagerly anticipated their independence, the change in status from a U.S. territory to a commonwealth immediately limited their ability to move freely between the two countries. Strict new limits allowed only fifty Filipinos to enter the United States each year. When the Philippines gained full independence, they would not be allowed to send any immigrants at all.

Filipinos in the United States had to make a hard choice when the new law went into effect. Since they were not U.S. citizens—and could not become citizens because they were not white—they would never be able to return to the Philippines to visit family if they chose to stay in America. If they did go home, chances are they would not be permitted back into the United States upon their return. Even so, the majority stayed in the United States. (The 1790 Naturalization Act prevented people of color from becoming naturalized citizens. The 1952 Immigration and Naturalization Act finally made all races eligible for naturalization.)

1945 to 1965

In 1941, Japan attacked Pearl Harbor, drawing the United States into World War II. Hours later, the Japanese attacked the American Air Force base in the Philippines. Thousands of Filipinos joined the United States armed forces to fight against the Japanese. In exchange, they were offered the chance to become U.S. citizens. Almost 11,000 took advantage of the opportunity to become the first *naturalized U.S. citizens* from the Philippines.

After World War II, the restrictions on immigration and citizenship for Filipinos were relaxed somewhat. Although the Philippines were now independent, they were allotted 100 visas each year. Any Filipino who had arrived in the United States before 1934 was allowed to become a naturalized citizen.

Unlike the first wave of immigrants, most of the Filipinos coming to America during this period were women. Some were wives of soldiers who had been stationed in the Philippines during World War II. Others were nurses who took part in advanced training programs and were invited to remain in the United States to work in inner-city hospitals and clinics. Neither the war brides nor the nurses were counted against the Philippines' annual quota of 100 immigrants. Filipino communities were established throughout the United States during this period.

Many of the Filipino men who immigrated to the United States immediately after World War II did so by enlisting in the Navy. These immigrants and their families settled in areas with large naval bases, such as San Diego, California; Norfolk, Virginia; and Honolulu, Hawaii.

After 1965

Further changes in U.S. immigration laws in 1965 resulted in a huge jump in immigration from the Philippines. In 1960, about 180,000 Filipinos lived in the United States. By 2000, over 2 million Filipinos and Filipino Americans called the United States their home.

Many of the Filipinos who immigrated to the United States after 1965 were looking for a better quality of life as well as more professional opportunities. Skilled workers made up about one-fourth of the Filipino immigrants who entered the United States during this time. Nearly all of the other immigrants were sponsored by family members. The West Coast continued to be a popular destination. Sizable communities also grew in urban areas such as New York City and Chicago. Unlike some immigrant groups that settle in a few locations, Filipinos live in every U.S. state.

Fast Facts

- Nearly every country in the world has a waiting list of unskilled workers wanting to immigrate to the United States. Only the Philippines and China have a backlog of skilled workers waiting for visas.

- Filipinos have one of the highest median incomes of all immigrant groups.

- Filipino immigrants tend to make more money than Filipino Americans.

- About one-third of Filipino Americans were under 20 in 1990.

Spotlight on
JOSIE NATORI

"Respect is the result of passion. I am a natural salesperson. I come from the Philippines, where being a woman entrepreneur is very commonplace. Women are always selling something from the time they are very young. It comes very natural to me."
    –Josie Natori, quoted in *Entrepreneur*

From Wall Street financier to fashion designer, Josie Natori has been very successful in the United States. Born in Manila, Philippines, in 1947, Natori attended college in America. By age twenty-seven, Natori worked as a vice president of investment banking at Merrill Lynch. Looking for more of a challenge, Natori considered opening her own business. She eventually decided to design clothing that would feature the traditional embroidery of the Philippines. When department store buyers suggested that she sell nightshirts instead of blouses, Natori's award-winning lingerie collection was born.

Twenty years later, Natori is founder and CEO of a flourishing fashion business. She has served as a commissioner to the White House Conference on Small Business. Her many awards include the Ellis Island Medal of Honor which recognizes the outstanding contributions of U.S. citizens, both native-born and naturalized.

Life in America

Filipinos have been creating a place for themselves in America for the past century. The earliest immigrants had to deal with open discrimination against Asians. More recent immigrants have encountered barriers of their own.

As the Filipino community grew larger, groups sharing a common interest or background formed organizations. These clubs provided friendship and a chance to maintain the Filipino culture while adapting to new lives. Some organizations taught traditional dances and music. Others set up study sessions to prepare immigrants for the citizenship test. Many organizations raised money for Filipino community centers in their adopted cities.

Filipino American organizations are just as important today. In many cases, the focus is on job advancement or charity. Passing along Filipino culture to American-born children remains a priority for many clubs.

With so many organizations to choose from, Filipino Americans can limit their socializing to people from their specific language group if they wish to. However, some Filipinos feel that splintering into so many groups isolates and divides the Filipino community. Since each group's needs come first, the overall political power of Filipino Americans is weakened.

Family

Filipino families generally have an easier time fitting into American life than many other immigrants. They come from an English-speaking, primarily Christian country. Cities like Manila are very Westernized. They have television, pop music, American clothing, and other contemporary cultural characteristics.

One of the biggest difficulties that Filipino parents face in the United States is the influence of other cultures on their children. In the Philippines, the emphasis is traditionally on fitting in and being part of the group. The needs of the family are much more important than an individual's wishes. People who fail to meet the expectations of the group bring shame to their family. In the Philippines, this pressure to honor one's family makes it easier for parents to discipline their children.

Filipino Pride

Over forty years ago, Fred and Dorothy Cordova organized Filipino Youth Activities (FYA) in Seattle, Washington. Although Filipino immigrants were known for starting cultural groups, this was one of the first formed by Filipino Americans. The founding parents were looking for activities that would challenge and entertain, yet teach their children about Filipino culture.

One of the first activities offered was the FYA Drill Team, whose members marched and danced in unison. Their routines required a lot of discipline and practice. Being chosen for the team was an honor. The drill team performed at parades and events in the Seattle area and was well received. As its reputation spread, the drill team began to tour nationally. Young people who participate in the FYA Drill Team usually become leaders in their communities as adults.

What started as a place to learn the language, dances, and martial arts of the Filipino culture has grown into a social-services agency. Filipino Youth Activities still offers classes in traditional dances, drill team, and eskima (a type of martial arts). It also reaches out to troubled youth who need an alternative to joining gangs.

But in the United States, the pressure isn't as great. When children don't obey their parents, they aren't shunned or ignored as they might be in the Philippines.

The worry over being shamed in the community causes other problems too. Parents often don't ask for help when their children start getting into trouble because that would bring shame to the family. With gang activity a serious problem in some areas, some parents choose to move to a new neighborhood rather than seek help from an outside source.

The owner of a seafood market in Virginia Beach, Virginia, packs fish in ice. His store is located in a shopping center in which nine out of ten businesses are owned by Filipinos.

Work

Filipinos are among the best-educated immigrants in the United States. They are well represented in professional and technical fields, especially health care, and as managers. As a result, Filipinos earn higher average salaries than most immigrants. This doesn't mean that all Filipinos are finding success in America. About one-third of the Filipino immigrants perform manual work and make much less than their fellow immigrants.

When looking at first- and second-generation employment, differences between Filipino-born immigrants and Filipino Americans begin to appear. The recent immigrants tend to be better educated and make more money than the American-born group. One possible explanation is that early Filipino immigrants tended to be employed in lower-paying jobs. Their children and grandchildren may not have been able to go to college or to get the extra training that higher-paying jobs require. Recent Filipino immigrants, on the other hand, often continue to work on advanced college degrees in their homeland until they receive their visas.

Spotlight on
Eduardo San Juan

Astronaut James Irwin salutes the American flag on the surface of the moon during the Apollo 15 *mission in August 1971. The lunar rover or "moon buggy," shown in the right corner of the photograph, was designed by Filipino engineer Eduardo San Juan.*

In the 1960s, the United States raced to put an astronaut on the moon before the Soviet Union. Colleges and universities added engineering courses, but the aircraft industries and the National Aeronautics and Space Administration (NASA) needed people to work on space designs immediately. They began hiring engineers from the Philippines, including a young man named Eduardo San Juan. While working at NASA, San Juan designed the lunar rover, a vehicle that astronauts used in order to study the surface of the moon. People called it the "moon buggy."

Later in his career, San Juan turned his attention to another unexplored frontier—the ocean. He worked to find ways for people to move around and conduct research under the sea.

School

Filipinos respect the advantages that a good education provides. It is not uncommon for all the children in a family to be professionals. In the Philippines, nearly everyone completes high school. About 42 percent finish college. In contrast, Filipino Americans have a high dropout rate in high school. Only 22 percent of Filipino Americans continue on to college. The differences in achievement by foreign-born parents and their American-born children are the source of conflict and tension for many families.

Some studies show that many Filipino girls receive conflicting messages about education. Parents encourage their daughters as well as their sons to excel in school and attend college. But they expect daughters to attend the nearest college so they can continue to live at home under parental supervision, while sons are encouraged to enroll in the best possible school regardless of location.

Religion

Like the population of many other former Spanish colonies, the majority of Filipinos are Roman Catholic, providing them with an easy transition to worship in America. Muslims and Protestants together make up less than 20 percent of the population.

Holidays and Festivals

Filipino immigrants in America continue to celebrate the independence movement, their religious beliefs and holidays, and family, just as they did in their homeland.

Celebrating Independence

Filipino Americans celebrate Philippine Independence Day on June 12 and Philippine-American Friendship Day on July 4. Programs include patriotic events and cultural programs, such as dances and martial arts exhibitions.

Among the holidays that are not religious, one of the most important is Rizal Day, held each December 30. José Rizal was a leader of the independence movement. Some communities have more than one celebration. Generally, the events include a dinner, music, the national anthem, and speeches.

Christian Holidays

The Roman Catholic calendar includes many Christian holidays which Filipino immigrants celebrate in much the same way as Americans. Filipinos often combine traditional and Catholic customs in their festivities. The Christmas season begins December 16. Masses, or church services, are held at the Catholic church before dawn. The last mass, on Christmas Eve, is held at midnight. Following the service, some families gather together for a feast called Noche Buena. Other families wait to have their special Christmas meal on Christmas Day.

Other important Christian celebrations are Easter and Flores de Mayo. During Flores de Mayo, people celebrate the gift of the spring rains by presenting fresh flowers and prayers to the Virgin Mary every day for a month. As Flores de Mayo draws to a close, members of the church take part in a procession called Santacruzan, which honors the finding of the Holy Cross, the cross on which Jesus was crucified. The Santacruzan is celebrated in Filipino American communities throughout the United States. Girls dressed in colorful dresses represent hope, faith, and other valued qualities. The girl representing Queen Helena, finder of the cross, walks under a canopy made of flowers. A float carrying the image of the Virgin Mary follows, along with a band. As the parade passes by, those watching from the street join the procession. Their lit candles brighten the evening as the group makes its way to the church for evening mass.

Muslim Holidays

Filipino Muslims in America continue to observe traditional Islamic holy days. They are based on a lunar calendar, so the actual date varies each year.

In the Islamic tradition, Ramadan (ROM-uh-don) is the most important month in the year. It is called the month of blessing. Muslims do not eat or drink from dawn until dusk during Ramadan. Prayer and works of charity are also important parts of this holiday.

As Ramadan ends, Muslims gather with family and friends to celebrate the feast of Eid al-Fitr. Children often get new clothes for the holiday, which usually lasts about three days.

Eid al-Adha (The Feast of the Sacrifice) teaches that Allah brings peace and happiness to those who do what He asks.

The Arts

Filipino American musicians are involved in all kinds of music, but a few remain faithful to their musical traditions. Traditional Filipino music is played on string instruments like guitars and the *git-git* and wind instruments made from bamboo. Drums and gongs carry the rhythm. Filipino musicians perform at festivals or in schools, introducing Americans to their culture. Other musicians create their own style of music by adding Filipino rhythms and instruments to pop music or jazz.

Traditional dance groups are probably the most visible way that Filipinos keep their heritage alive. Cultural festivals and community events often feature performances of *tinikling* or *singkil*. Many Americans are familiar with tinikling, a dance from the Visayan region. Dancers step quickly and gracefully between tapping poles, imitating the movements of the *tinikling* bird stepping over sticks and grass. The dance was incorporated into many elementary school physical education programs in the 1960s and 1970s. The *singkil* dance is one of the oldest Filipino dances, originating on the southern island of Mindanao. In the Garden *Singkil,* the dancers retell the story of Princess Gandingan's encounter with butterflies in her garden. Royal princesses in the Mindanao region are still required to learn this dance today.

Children from the Filipiniana Dance Troupe in traditional Filipino dress prepare to perform a putong or "welcome dance" at the opening of the Filipino Community Center in Honolulu, Hawaii. The community center is the largest such center outside of the Philippines.

Food

Filipino families can find all the ingredients they need for their traditional foods in the United States. They usually prepare simple noodle dishes or stews for daily meals. American foods are also popular. Filipinos can also enjoy traditional foods without having to cook themselves. The number of Filipino restaurants is growing steadily. Many grocery stores in California sell frozen Filipino foods and mixes.

The food of the Philippines shows the influence of its many cultures. Favorite foods and spices from Malaysia, Spain, Mexico, and China flavor the dishes. The cooking styles also reflect different cultures.

Lechon, adobo, and *lumpia* are all considered national dishes of the Philippines. *Lechon* is a whole roasted pig, served only on special occasions such as holidays or festivals. *Adobo* is a stew made of pork, chicken, or seafood, cooked in a sauce of vinegar, soy sauce, garlic, and pepper. *Lumpia* are Filipino egg rolls. Desserts are usually very sweet. Most are made with coconut.

Recipe

Chicken Adobo in Coconut Milk

2 tablespoons garlic, minced

1 onion, chopped

2 tablespoons olive oil

1 whole chicken, cut into 8 to 10 pieces

3 cups coconut milk

1 teaspoon ground black pepper

1 teaspoon salt

1 teaspoon fresh ginger, grated

3 tablespoons vinegar

1 small piece chili (optional)

In a soup pot, sauté the garlic and onion in the olive oil over medium heat. Add chicken pieces, 2 cups of coconut milk, black pepper, salt, ginger, and vinegar. Bring to a boil and simmer uncovered until chicken is very tender, about 1 hour and 10 minutes. Add chili if you want a hot and spicy dish. Add remaining coconut milk, stir, and simmer 2 to 3 minutes until sauce is thick and oily. Serve hot over rice.

NOTE: Coconut milk is found in Hispanic or Asian food markets in canned or powdered forms. If using powdered form, follow package instructions to make coconut milk.

Source: Pacific Crossings *by Lily Gamboa O'Boyle*

CHAPTER FOUR

Ghanaians

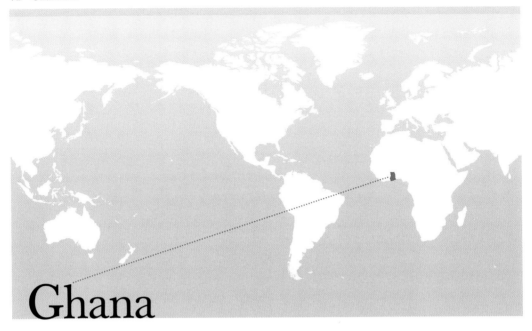

Ghana

and the United States share a long history. The first link—slavery—was a tragic one. Many of the slaves that were brought to colonial America came from West Africa, including Ghana. After the slave trade ended, Ghana became a British *colony* called the Gold Coast.

When Ghana became an independent nation in 1957, ties with the United States grew stronger. Ghana was the first country to welcome Peace Corps volunteers. The program in Ghana quickly grew into one of the largest Peace Corps programs in the world. Volunteers continue to provide help with education, farming, health care, and small business development.

Many African Americans view Ghana as a symbol of their heritage and culture. During the civil rights movement, African Americans were inspired by Ghana's successful drive for independence. A growing tourism industry in Ghana builds upon these connections.

With the Internet's arrival some American high-tech companies are starting to set up support centers in Ghana. Until recently, when people in New York City got a ticket for playing their music too loud or for littering, a copy of the ticket was sent to Ghana. Workers in Ghana entered information from tickets into a computer database and sent it back to the city.

With increasing contact between the two nations, Ghanaians began moving to the United States. Numbers were limited at first by strict laws. These laws were changed in 1965 and again in 1995. Today, Ghanaians and other West Africans make up one of the fastest growing immigrant groups in America.

A Quick Look Back

People have been living in what is now Ghana for about 3,500 years. But it was gold that brought Ghana to the attention of European countries in 1471. They called the region the Gold Coast and set up trading posts to buy and sell gold. Later, the same traders bought and sold slaves. About 150 years later, Ghana stood as a symbol of African pride when it became the first country in sub-Saharan Africa to win independence from European colonists.

Early History

Around the tenth century, the first kingdom in West Africa became very strong. It was called the Kingdom of Ghana but had no relation to the modern nation of Ghana other than sharing a name. As the kingdom expanded and was taken over by other rulers, people started to move south into what is now the country of Ghana to avoid the inevitable conflicts.

People settling in this southern area traded gold and kola nuts with the kingdoms to the north. Many of the traders who came to the area were Muslim. They introduced Islam to the people living there. Today, most of the Gonja (GONE-yah) and Dagomba people who live in the northern part of Ghana are Muslim.

Fast Facts

• Ghana was the first African country to gain its independence from a European power.

• In 1994, Ghana became the first West African country to be connected to the Internet.

• Ghana is one of the top sources of gold in the world. In 2000, over 150,000 pounds (67,500 kilograms) of gold were mined.

• The sale of cacao, the beans from which chocolate is made, brings in almost as much money as the gold.

Slave Trade

In 1471, the Portuguese arrived in Ghana. They set up trading centers with the African people in the region, exchanging guns and slaves for gold dust.

Before long, traders from Spain, Italy, Denmark, Holland, and Britain arrived in the Gold Coast region. The traders fought each other throughout the 1600s, trying to gain control of the area. By the 1700s, the British, Dutch, and Danish traders controlled the area. Instead of trading for gold, they now traded for slaves. The native people of the region often brought in their prisoners of war and sold them to the slave traders for guns and ammunition. Sometimes tribal groups went to other areas and captured people to be sold as slaves. People who had broken laws or customs were also sent into slavery.

Hundreds of thousands of slaves were imprisoned in the slave fortress in Cape Coast, Ghana, and then loaded on slave ships and sent to America and Europe. Recently, conservationists have restored the castle and turned it into a museum.

The slave trade continued for over a hundred years. In 1807, Britain became the first country to stop buying and selling slaves in Ghana. Before long, other countries did the same. Slowly, the era of slave trading came to an end.

A British Colony

Britain understood that, even without the slave trade, Ghana was still very valuable. It had many products that could be used in the new factories that were being built in Britain. In order to get the products, the British needed to control the area and keep it peaceful.

Through a combination of force and diplomacy, Britain controlled most of the coastal region of Ghana by the early 1800s. The Ashanti kingdom ruled much of the central region. Throughout the rest of the century, these two powers battled each other for control. The British signed *treaties* with enemies of the Ashanti. They also bought the coastal areas that had been settled by Denmark and Holland. Finally, by 1902, the British controlled all of Ghana. They called it the Gold Coast Colony.

Moving toward Independence

Under British rule, miles of railroads were built in the colony. Schools were also built. Most of them were run by missionaries, people who introduce Christianity to other people. Gradually, Ghanaians gained more power in the colonial government.

These changes were good, but the population wanted true independence. Kwame Nkrumah (n-KROO-mah), an African who had gone to school in America, became a leader of the independence movement. In 1950, Nkrumah led boycotts and strikes against businesses and the government. This resistance upset the British, who arrested Nkrumah and other leaders. While they were in prison, other members of the movement continued Nkrumah's work.

A year later, many people from Nkrumah's party were elected as legislative representatives. The governor of the colony let Nkrumah out of jail and asked Nkrumah to be the prime minister of the Gold Coast. He accepted and was later elected to the position.

A New Country

Ghana's first president, Kwame Nkrumah, is pictured at the United Nations headquarters in New York City in 1961.

In 1957, the Gold Coast Colony won its independence from Great Britain. Nkrumah and other leaders changed the name of the country to Ghana, after the first great empire in West Africa.

Nkrumah worked hard to improve the lives of people in Ghana. He also supported other African countries that were trying to win their independence. But he also helped pass new laws that gave him more power. Nkrumah often used these laws to keep people from criticizing him or his government. He thought that the only way for Ghana to remain strong was for the people to show a united front.

When the *economy* stopped growing, people had trouble making a living. They blamed Nkrumah's policies. So, in 1966, the military led a *coup* that forced Nkrumah from office. The military leaders changed the *constitution* to allow for democratic elections between multiple political parties. Three years later, Kofi Busia (KOH-fee BOO-see-ah) was elected prime minister of Ghana. But the economy continued to stagnate and Busia was overthrown in a military coup in 1972.

Turmoil and Conflict

Political upheaval and violence continued throughout the next decade. In the late 1970s, Lieutenant Jerry John Rawlings took control of the president's office. The economy, which had been bad, got even worse in the 1980s. People started leaving Ghana by the thousands. Unskilled Ghanaian workers who had gone to Nigeria hoping to find jobs were forced to leave the country a few years later. The Nigerian government claimed that Ghanaians were not only involved in crime; but were taking jobs away from Nigerians. As a result, some Ghanaians began immigrating to the United States.

In 1983, Rawlings met with people from the International Monetary Fund (IMF). The IMF is a United Nations group that helps countries improve their economies. The changes that the IMF and Rawlings agreed upon did help Ghana's economy grow.

Rawlings also instituted changes that made Ghana more democratic. Presidential elections were held in 1992 and Rawlings was elected president. Although he first ruled as a virtual dictator, in recent years Rawlings has been widely praised for bringing stability and economic growth to Ghana.

Jerry Rawlings was the first president in Ghana's history to transfer power peacefully to a new elected leader.

Ghana Today

Ghana continued to grow stronger through the 1990s. Businesses were started and more jobs were created. The government made museums out of forts that had been slave-trading centers. It also began celebrating the end of slavery on August 1. Both of these actions have drawn tourists from America and other nations.

In January 2001, President Rawlings stepped down and John Kufuor took office as the president-elect of Ghana. This marked the first time in Ghana's history that the presidency changed hands peacefully.

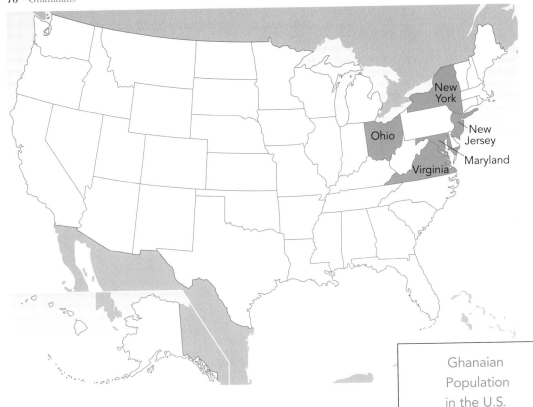

Ghanaian Population in the U.S.	
New York	19,251
Maryland	5,005
New Jersey	3,211
Ohio	2,490
Virginia	2,093

Source: U.S. Census, 2000

Coming to America

The first Africans to come to the United States were unwilling immigrants. For nearly 300 years they had been captured in Ghana and other African nations and sold to work as slaves far from their homelands. Even after slavery ended in 1865, racist feelings remained throughout much of America. Few Africans wanted to move permanently to a country that thought of them as inferior. In the early 1900s, some Africans did come to the United States to attend college. Among them was Ghana's first leader, Kwame Nkrumah.

The American civil rights movement in the 1960s led to more opportunities for African Americans. But the number of immigrants from Ghana stayed low. U.S. laws limited the number of Africans who could

U.S./Ghanaian Immigration by Decade

Decade	Immigrants
1971–80	5,195
1981–90	14,876
1991–2000	35,638

Source: Statistical Yearbook of the Immigration and Naturalization Service

immigrate each year, but the air of hope in Ghana at that time may have had a bigger influence on its citizens. After gaining independence in 1957, Ghanaians were excited about building their own country.

The number of Ghanaians who immigrated to the United States each year didn't show a big jump until the late 1970s. This followed several changes in the government of Ghana. The economy was getting worse each year. By the mid-1980s, over 1,000 Ghanaians were arriving in the United States each year. Most of these immigrants sought better living conditions and opportunities.

The next wave of immigrants came after the *diversity lottery* program started in 1995. This program gives extra visas to countries that had not sent many immigrants to the United States in the past. The diversity lottery accounts for roughly half of the immigrants from Ghana in recent years. Nearly all of the other Ghanaians are admitted through the programs that bring family members of U.S. residents and citizens to this country.

According to the U.S. Census in 2000, most Ghanaians have settled along the east coast of the United States. They are one of the fastest growing immigrant groups there. Other communities have formed in major cities across the United States. Ghanaians actively keep their culture and language alive through ethnic clubs such as the Asanteman Kuo, the Ewe Association, the Volta Club, and the Ga-Adangbe Association.

Although they are making new homes in the United States, most Ghanaians still keep close ties with their home country. They often send money back to family members. They also work to improve life in Ghana, raising money to pay for medical care, schools, and other needs.

Ghanaians in NYC

In recent years, about 1,600 Ghanaians have settled in New York City each year. This represents a 380 percent increase from the mid- to late 1990s.

Did you know?

In 1995, Ghana's President Rawlings announced a plan that would offer Ghanaian citizenship to African Americans, allowing them to claim citizenship in both America and Ghana. So far, the law has not been passed.

Even without dual citizenship, some African Americans have claimed Ghana as their homeland. They are moving to Ghana, buying land, and making plans to settle there permanently.

Life in America

Family

The extended family is very important in Ghana. Children are raised not just by parents, but by grandparents, aunts, and uncles. When the first immigrants arrived in America, they usually came with just their immediate family. Cultural associations helped fill the gap, providing support for parents and children. Children and adults were able to continue their cultural traditions.

Parents continue to worry about the effect of American culture on their children. West African families stress respect and discipline, values that sometimes seem to be missing in their American neighborhoods. More and more parents are joining together to set up culture schools that children attend after regular school or on weekends. Students may learn a traditional language or dances during the lessons, or they may receive help with their homework. Most importantly, the values that are honored in their culture are reinforced. For some parents, sending their children back to Ghana to be raised in a traditional setting is a last resort.

Work

Since English is the official language of Ghana, most immigrants have a head start in the U.S. job market. Several things can make finding a job more difficult, though. Many educated Ghanaians find that they are required to complete extra schooling or take exams in order to continue to work in their chosen fields. With a family to support, they may not have the time or money to do this. As a result, they often take jobs for which they are overqualified.

Another problem that affects immigrants from Ghana is the difference in technology between the two countries. Most of the better-paying jobs in the United States require experience with computers. Few people in Ghana can afford a computer, though. One hour of Internet access at an Internet café can cost as much as most people make for a day's work.

For many Ghanaians, starting their own business is the answer to these problems. Their businesses appeal to both fellow immigrants and to African Americans. Some Ghanaian immigrants cook traditional foods for special events, offer hair-braiding, or open grocery stores that sell ingredients from Ghana. Others sell traditional clothing or music.

Women in Ghana have a long tradition of buying and selling products to make money for their families. They brought food and other goods to markets to trade or sell. Some women bought produce in rural areas and resold it in the city markets. Those women who work in professional careers are generally paid the same amount as men in their fields.

Spotlight on
PETER PIPIM

Long ago, people told stories to explain how a custom got started or why people act in a certain way. Folktales like these help us understand other cultures and what they value.

Peter Pipim, an educational specialist from Ghana, shares the stories of his country with visitors to the Smithsonian Institution's National Museum of African Art in Washington, D.C. He also sets up exhibits that show the art and history of Ghana and other African countries.

Pipim won the Smithsonian Unsung Hero Award for his work at the museum. The people he works with note that he teaches sensitivity and honor and the need to do your best.

School

Ghanaian students have much the same experience as other immigrants in American schools. Those who know English, depending upon their age and educational level, fare better than the younger children who did most of their primary lessons in their native language. However, they still may have a hard time fitting in. They often have to deal with racism from both white and African American classmates.

Ghanaian girls have an advantage in America compared to girls back home. Most of the students in Ghana are male, increasingly so in upper grades. Females often marry at a young age and drop out of school. This practice is not encouraged among the immigrants who move here, allowing girls to complete high school and even move on to higher education.

Religion

As Ghanaians move to the United States, they bring their religious practices with them. There are three main religions in Ghana: traditional religions, Christianity, and Islam.

Traditional Religions

Nearly half of the people in Ghana practice the traditional religions of their ethnic groups. These religions share some common ideas. In each, there is one Supreme Being or god. There are also several other gods that live in rivers, trees, and mountains. People pray to these gods, asking them to carry the message to the Supreme Being.

Spirits, including spirits of ancestors, are also important in the traditional religions. People celebrate and honor their ancestors to strengthen their relations with the spirits.

Christianity

The missionaries who accompanied the European colonists to the Gold Coast introduced Christianity to the people living in the southern part of Ghana. Presbyterians, Methodists, Roman Catholics, and Evangelical Presbyterians set up missions and schools, hoping that students would continue to worship in that faith.

The fastest growing churches in Ghana are Apostolic and Pentecostal. They combine traditional beliefs with Christianity. There is a strong belief in magic, including chants and charms that can fight off evil forces. Churches of the same faith are found in the United States. Many Ghanaian communities have adapted the church buildings and customs to include those from home. Hearing the same songs and seeing the same decorations help new immigrants feel at home. The social side of these churches, which often sponsor drum societies and singing groups, appeals to many young people.

Religions of Ghana

a Traditional 38%
b Islam 30%
c Christianity 24%
d Other 8%

Source: CIA World Factbook, *2002*

Islam

The earliest organized religion to be introduced to Ghana was Islam. Traders from the north were primarily Muslim. When they brought goods to trade for gold, they would share their religion with the people in that area.

Most Ghanaian Muslims are followers of Sunni Islam. Unlike Muslims and Christians in other countries, those in Ghana have lived together peacefully for years.

Holidays and Festivals

The official holiday calendar for Ghana looks much like that of the United States. Businesses are closed for the celebration of the New Year, Easter, Christmas, and the Muslim holidays of Eid al-Fitr and Eid al-Adha. In addition to the

Muslim immigrants from Ghana and other countries continue to practice their religion in the United States. In this photograph, a group of several thousand Muslim men face Mecca and bow in prayer at New York's Coney Island to mark the holiday of Eid al-Adha.

traditional religious holidays, Ghanaians celebrate many traditional festivals. At least two of these festivals are celebrated in the United States by the Ghanaian community.

Odwira (Durbar)

Odwira is a time set aside in the fall to give thanks to the gods for all their blessings. It is also a time to gather with family, honor ancestors, and strengthen bonds. Prayers are offered for the land and for the people.

During Odwira, the Akan people also honor and meet with their leaders. Dressed in the traditional kente cloth that represents royalty, the chiefs and queens are carried in a procession. Ceremonial umbrellas represent the protection offered by the chiefs and queens. Drummers, dancers, and singers offer tribute to the leaders.

In the United States, associations such as the Asanteman Kuo hold similar ceremonies every three years when new leaders take office. The chiefs and queen mothers of the associations across North America wear traditional ceremonial clothing and gold and silver jewelry. Drummers, dancers, and singers lead the procession under the ceremonial umbrellas. In America, a durbar can last all day. Just like the festival in Ghana, it brings the Ashanti community together and builds a sense of belonging.

Obo Addy

Obo Addy's contributions to folk and traditional art were recognized by the National Endowment for the Arts in 1996 when he received a National Heritage Fellowship. Growing up in Ghana, Addy was named a "master drummer" at age six. He and his brothers performed at the Olympic Games in Munich, Germany, in 1972. He moved to the United States in 1978. He performs and teaches traditional tribal and Highlife music.

Homowo

The Ga-Adangbe people rejoice throughout August with feasts, dances, and processions. The month ends with a celebration of Homowo, meaning "hunger go to sleep." During this harvest festival, people parade through the streets. They sprinkle cornmeal everywhere to feed the ancestors. Special meals of fish and palm nut soup are served during Homowo.

Obo Addy, a drummer from Ghana, has organized a Homowo festival in Portland, Oregon. The weeklong festival includes a royal procession, dances, prayers, and music.

The Arts

The people of Ghana have many traditional art forms, including music and dance, carving, and jewelry making. They are most known for their unique Highlife music (a blend of African, European, and Caribbean music) and the royal kente cloth.

Kente Cloth

Kente cloth, the brightly colored traditional fabric of the Ashanti people, has always been associated with royalty and ceremony in Ghana. During the civil rights movement in the United States, it became a powerful symbol of African Americans' pride in their cultural heritage. Today, kente patterns are seen on everything from bandages to Barbie dolls, sparking a debate on kente's role in modern life.

Traditional kente cloth is usually woven by men. They use silk to create strips of cloth 3 or 4 inches (7.5 or 10 centimeters) wide. The strips are then sewn together to make a robe, headdress, or other garment. Each color used in kente has a meaning, as do the patterns. Weavers, who have trained for years, create symbolic patterns for each garment they make.

Members of the Ishangi Family African Dancers perform a dance from their native Ghana to celebrate World Refugee Day on Ellis Island in New York Harbor.

The patterns are not recorded anywhere; the weaver memorizes the patterns or re-creates one from a sample.

This swatch of kente cloth shows the traditional striped pattern.

In Africa, kente has a ceremonial role. It is worn only on special occasions, such as durbars. When Nkrumah became the prime minister of Ghana, he wore kente robes to emphasize his role as the leader of the country. Many African Americans adopted kente as a symbol of their fight for equal rights.

Many people feel that the only appropriate use of kente is for African ceremonies. Others think that the widespread use of the patterns shows how popular kente has become as a symbol of Africa. Museum and art exhibits have brought the question before the public, but the debate still continues.

Highlife Music

Early in the twentieth century, musicians in Ghana began combining musical styles. Music from Africa, Europe, and the Caribbean was blended to create a new sound called Highlife. Bands used instruments ranging from African drums to guitars and accordions, depending on whether they were playing the ballroom or rural style Highlife. Highlife continued to change, with swing and big band sounds being added in the 1940s. By the 1950s and 1960s, Highlife was very popular in dance clubs. Today, Highlife has a reggae flavor that combines with its traditional roots. It remains one of the most popular musical styles in Africa.

Food

Stews are a mainstay of the Ghanaian diet. They may have many different kinds of vegetables, along with fish or chicken. These stews are usually served with *fufu,* a starchy dish that is popular throughout Ghana and West Africa. *Fufu* can be made from yams, cassava, or plantain. Usually, people in the northern part of Ghana use yams, while people in the south make *fufu* from cassava or plantain. In America, *fufu* can be made by beating and stirring the boiled yams or cassava or by using convenience foods such as instant potato flakes or biscuit mix in place of the vegetables.

These men are making fufu *by pounding yams or cassava with large mallets to make a starchy paste.*

Peanut Soup with Chicken

2 pounds chicken, cut into pieces

salt and pepper

2 large onions, finely chopped

1 13-ounce can of tomatoes

Heaping 1/2 cup peanut butter

7 cups boiling water

2 to 3 small red chili peppers, seeded and finely chopped

4 to 8 mushrooms

2 pounds cooked fish fillets (salted, smoked, grilled, fried, or dried)

Season the chicken with salt and pepper and place in a very large, heavy saucepan. Add the chopped onions and cook together on medium heat, stirring constantly, until the outside of the meat is "sealed" or slightly cooked.

Blend the canned tomatoes to a smooth consistency, then pour into the meat and onion mixture. Stir and allow to simmer.

In a large bowl, combine the peanut butter and 1 1/2 cups of the boiling water. With a wooden spoon, blend together until the mixture is a creamy, smooth sauce. (This can also be done in a blender or food processor.) Add to the meat and tomato mixture, along with the chilies and mushrooms. Mix well, then stir in the rest of the water and the cooked fish, and simmer for an additional 30 minutes on medium heat, until the chicken is fully cooked and the soup somewhat thickened and reduced.

Serve hot over *fufu*. Serves 4.

Source: I Was Never Here and This Never Happened
by Dorinda Hafner

CHAPTER FIVE

Guatemalans

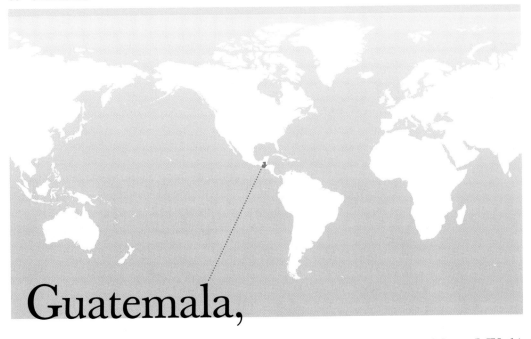

Guatemala,

a large country south of Mexico, is home to the Maya (MY-ah) people, whose ancestors created one of the most fascinating ancient cultures in the world. Over the years, Spanish *conquerors,* African slaves, German planters, and American businesses have come to Guatemala as well.

Extreme discrimination against the Maya by the Spanish and their *descendants* led to the development of one of the most uneven divisions of wealth in the region. Soon after the Spanish conquered Guatemala in the sixteenth century, a small group of Europeans and Ladinos (people with both European and Maya ancestors) owned most of the land. They also controlled most of the money.

This unfair system set the stage for a brutal *civil war* that started in 1960. Torn apart by thirty-six years of civil war, Guatemala is struggling today to rebuild. Some refugees who left the country during the war are returning to their villages. The future of this beautiful country depends upon the willingness of Guatemalans to end centuries of discrimination and the abuse of power by the military.

Ethnic Groups
of Guatemala

a Ladino 55%

b Amerindian 43%

c white/other 2%

Source: CIA
World Factbook, *2002*

A Quick Look Back

The Maya, one of the most interesting and advanced *civilizations* in the Americas began in the highlands of Guatemala. The Maya people built a strong government of city-states, independent cities that ruled their surrounding areas. Ceremonial cities with giant pyramids were constructed without the use of animals or wheeled vehicles to move the stones.

The Maya's talents were not limited to building. The calendar that they created after studying the stars and planets is as accurate as calendars today. They created a written language—the only real writing system developed in the Americas—by carving picture symbols into rock. They also developed a mathematical system.

The Mayans built pyramids such as this in Guatemala between A.D. 300 and 900.

For unknown reasons, most of the Maya left their cities in Guatemala around A.D. 900. They moved north to Mexico, where more pyramids and cities were built. The Maya who stayed in Guatemala included the Quiché (kee-chay) and Cakchiquel people. They were almost completely destroyed by Spanish invaders, but some survived. Their descendants still live in Guatemala today. They are often called *indigenous,* or native, people.

Spanish Rule

Spain invaded Guatemala in 1524 and turned the Maya people into slaves. Their religion and languages were outlawed. Over the next century, nearly all the Maya died in slavery or from diseases the Spanish brought.

The Spanish called their new colony the Kingdom of Guatemala. It included much of Central America. In 1786, the kingdom was split into five provinces: Guatemala, El Salvador, Chiapas (Mexico), Honduras, and Nicaragua.

Independence from Spain

Colonists in Mexico and Central America began working for independence from Spain in the early 1800s. The provinces were gradually given more rights to govern themselves and gained their independence without a war.

Mexico was the first to declare independence from Spain. Months later, in 1821, Guatemala did the same. Eventually, Guatemala, El Salvador, Honduras, Costa Rica, and Nicaragua joined together to form the United Provinces of Central America. This federation lasted nearly twenty years. It caused bitterness and resentment among the people, many of whom lost their lands and businesses. The Catholic Church also lost much of its land and power. *Guerrillas* led by Rafael Carrera began staging revolts against the government.

Republic of Guatemala

The guerrilla war brought the United Provinces federation to an end in 1840. Carrera assumed control of Guatemala and ruled as a dictator, returning power to the Catholic Church and initiating the export of coffee and other products.

Liberal leaders seized control of Guatemala's government in 1871, the first in a series of liberal dictators that would rule until 1944. Their emphasis on economic growth expanded the coffee industry and brought in money to build roads and other improvements. Many people became wealthy. But the rural people remained very poor and the government did little to help them.

The Catholic Church was greatly affected during this period. Education, which had been the responsibility of the Church, was placed under the direction of the government. The number of priests was sharply limited. The Church lost much of the land it owned as well. Once again, rural Guatemalans bore the brunt of these changes. Most lost their only chance at education when the priests were forced to leave.

The 1900s

As the new century began, Guatemala's growth continued. President Manuel Estrada Cabrera welcomed foreign investment. American-owned companies, especially the United Fruit Company (UFCO), built huge banana plantations. At the same time, Germans started to control the coffee trade. Cabrera's government offered the foreigners lots of land and low taxes. UFCO built miles of railroads and seaports to make it easier to ship its products to other countries. Although the foreign companies created jobs, many Guatemalans resented the foreigners who controlled so much of the country. The company began to work very closely with the dictators who ruled Guatemala. It seemed as if UFCO was involved in every deal the government made.

President Cabrera's time in office was marked by corruption. Resentment against his actions grew, and he was overthrown in a coup in 1920. Military leaders affiliated with the liberal party ruled for the next ten years. They allowed some political freedom, including the ability to organize labor unions that pushed for better pay and working conditions. However, they stopped any attempt by the workers to gain real political power.

In 1931 President Jorge Ubico Castaneda took office. His government worked with the coffee growers and UFCO to stop the workers from rebelling. Ubico accused his critics of being Communists; many were executed or sent into exile. He made poor people work on government projects such as building roads or putting up telegraph lines.

When World War II broke out, Ubico recognized that Guatemala's relationship with the United States was far more important than its ties to Germany. Guatemala declared war on Germany in 1941 and fought with the United States and the Allies in World War II. At home, Guatemalans continued to press for a more democratic government. The election of Juan José Arévalo in 1944 promised to be a step in that direction.

A banner of the General Confederation of Workers, Guatemala's major labor union, hangs from the United Fruit Company's hiring hall in Puerto Barrios in 1954. At that time, Guatemala's labor unions were locked in a struggle with UFCO over the rights of workers to organize into unions.

Ten Years of Spring

One of Arévalo's first tasks was to create a new *constitution*. The new laws gave rich people and foreigners fewer advantages. Freedom of speech and freedom of the press were protected. Women were given the right to vote, and labor unions and political parties were allowed to organize. The majority of Guatemalans, mostly the poor and working class, were in favor of these changes. They were hopeful that improved health care and opportunities to go to school would help their children lead better lives. Wealthy people, however, felt threatened by the new laws. The Roman Catholic Church didn't like the limits on its political activity. Planters and businesses like UFCO didn't want to deal with the labor unions or pay higher wages. They began to lead the United States into thinking that the new government favored Communism.

In 1951, Jacobo Arbenz Guzmán was elected president. He expanded the programs that Arévalo had begun. In the spirit of democracy, he allowed more political parties to form, including the Communist party. He also started a land reform program. This program allowed the government to purchase land that was not being used by the large plantations. The payments were based on the value the owners had declared on their tax records. The government then would sell the land at low prices to rural people whose land had been taken away decades earlier.

This program greatly affected UFCO. They claimed their land was worth more than the Guatemalan government wanted to pay. In retaliation, UFCO complained to the U.S. government that Communists in Guatemala were becoming very powerful. The United States, in the midst of the Cold War against the spread of Communism, responded by training a group of Guatemalan *exiles* and supporting their efforts to take control of Guatemala.

Military Rule

The United States helped train former Guatemalan military officers to overthrow President Arbenz in 1954. It gave them money and weapons, helped them invade Guatemala and take over the government, and then supported their efforts through much of the civil war that followed. Castillo Armas, the leader of the exiles, took over as president.

The new military government did away with many of the reforms that Arévalo and Arbenz had established. Freedom of speech was limited. Land was returned to the previous wealthy landowners and businesses. The military grew more powerful than ever before. Many of the officers took money illegally and became very rich.

Ordinary people didn't have any power or representation in the government to make a change. The leaders listened to people with money, and most Guatemalans were poor. The only way they could make the government pay attention to them was through violence. By 1960 guerrilla groups, led by middle-class students and intellectuals who had supported Arbenz's reforms, joined together to form the Rebel Armed Forces (known by the Spanish acronym FAR). The longest civil war in the Western Hemisphere was beginning.

Civil War

Over the next thirty years, the military controlled Guatemala. This was true whether an army officer or a civilian was president. In the late 1960s, death squads began killing anyone who spoke out against the government. The military continued the civil war against FAR's guerrilla forces.

As the war went on, the guerrilla groups banded together to form the Guatemalan National Revolutionary Unity (known by the Spanish acronym URNG). The guerrillas were popular with many rural people. But often the people were trapped between the two sides. The military tortured or killed anyone suspected of helping the guerrillas. The guerrillas threatened anyone who they thought was helping the government. From 1978 until 1982, about 1,000 people were killed each month. A new guerrilla group, the Guerrilla Army of the Poor, emerged during this time. It was the first group to actively recruit the rural poor, most of them Maya.

The dictator in office in 1982, Ríos Montt, tried to end the civil war but wasn't able to reach an agreement with the URNG. In retaliation, Ríos Montt implemented a violent program to end its resistance. He ordered the villagers who lived in rural areas to fight against the guerrillas. At the same time, he ordered the army to destroy any people or villages that helped the guerrillas. This program was known as the scorched earth policy.

During this program, thousands of native people were killed. Many others "disappeared," probably tortured, killed, and buried in hidden graves. Thousands more fled from their homes. Most went to Mexico. Some of them continued on to the United States. Over 400 Maya villages were destroyed; some were burned to the ground.

Young rebels in the URNG listen to a tape of Guatemalan history at their mountain base near Esquintla in this 1996 photo. The rebel army began educating its troops in order to make the transition from a military to a political force after the final peace agreement was signed.

Slowly the world became aware of the atrocities in Guatemala. International groups spoke out against the government's actions. Tourism, once an important source of Guatemala's income, was slowing because of the violence.

In the face of mounting international pressure, the military finally turned over some power to civilians in 1985. Marco Vinicio Cerezo was elected president. He was not able to end the civil war, but he did set the foundation for peace when he and the leaders of El Salvador, Nicaragua, Honduras, and Costa Rica signed the Central American Peace Accord of 1987. This agreement said that all five countries would work to achieve freedom of expression and democratic elections, they would release political prisoners, and they would refuse to accept military aid from or provide military aid to foreign countries.

Ending of the Civil War

President Alvaro Arzú Irigoyen (left) ordered the Guatemalan army to cease hostilities against leftist guerrillas in 1996.

Although the military no longer ran the country, there were constant reports of killings and torture by the military throughout the late 1980s. Claims that the U.S. government secretly continued to support the Guatemalan military have been investigated by Congress and the UN. There is evidence that the U.S. government helped cover up the human rights abuses by the military in Guatemala, but there has been little punishment for those involved.

The Guatemalan government and the guerrilla forces began talking about a peace agreement in the early 1990s. When Alvaro Arzú Irigoyen became president in 1996, the peace plan became his main concern. He met with the guerrilla leaders. He got rid of corrupt leaders in the military and the police. Finally, on December 29, 1996, a peace agreement was signed.

The peace agreement had several requirements. One was that the guerrillas had to give up their weapons. Another was that Guatemala had to reduce its army. One of the most important requirements was that the Guatemalan government put an end to centuries of discrimination against the Maya and their culture.

Guatemala Today

As the twenty-first century begins, Guatemala is struggling to move toward democracy. There is still a huge gap between the rich and the poor. The army doesn't have as much influence over government policy as it did in the past, but its leaders still involve themselves in governmental matters at times, rather than national defense. By mid-2002, there were reports of increasing corruption in the government. Many groups fear that the 1996 peace agreement is in danger of being ignored.

As part of the peace agreement, the UN agreed to investigate the human rights abuses that took place during the civil war. The UN's Truth Commission released its final report on the Guatemalan civil war in 1999. The report stated that the Guatemalan army was responsible for about 93 percent of the war crimes, including over 600 massacres. The guerrilla forces committed about 3 percent of the human rights abuses. The commission also found that the United States was partly to blame for its support of Guatemala's military with money and training.

The Guatemalan Civil War

The Guatemalan civil war lasted thirty-six years. During that time, about 200,000 people were killed or disappeared, 440 Maya villages were destroyed, and 1 million people had to leave their homes.

The chief of Guatemala's Historic Clarification Commission, also known as the Truth Commission, contemplates the 590 crosses in a chapel in Bebaj that are dedicated to the victims of violence during Guatemala's thirty-six-year civil war.

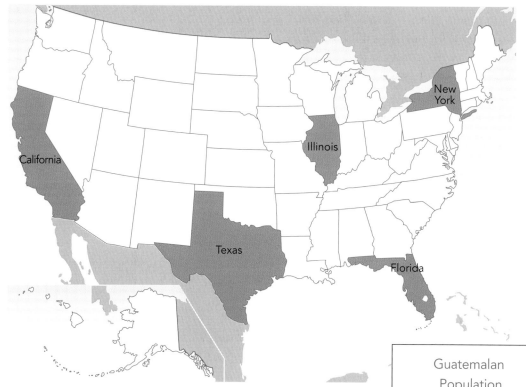

Coming to America

Guatemalan Population in the U.S.	
California	216,894
Florida	48,686
Illinois	30,193
New York	29,245
Texas	25,226

Source: U.S. Census, 2000

T housands of Guatemalans have come to the United States in recent years. Many were fleeing the terror of the civil war that was destroying their country. Others, their livelihoods crippled by the effects of the war, sought steady work so they could support their families.

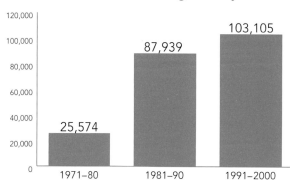

U.S./Guatemalan Immigration by Decade

Source: Statistical Yearbook of the Immigration and Naturalization Service

Few Guatemalans were granted *asylum* in the United States until the 1990s. In part, this was because few people outside of Guatemala knew how horrible the situation had become for the rural people caught between the military groups and the guerrillas. In addition, because the United States supported the Guatemalan government through much of the civil war, people who left Guatemala were often assumed to be ineligible for asylum.

This does not mean that refugees from Guatemala didn't come to the United States. Many just entered the country illegally rather than arriving as officially recognized and supported refugees or asylum seekers. By 1996, the Immigration and Naturalization Service estimated that 165,000 Guatemalans were living illegally in the United States.

Most Guatemalans have settled in areas that have a high concentration of industry or farm work. Southern California, with both, has the largest number of Guatemalans. Large Guatemalan communities are also found in south Florida, Illinois, New York, and Texas.

Life in America

For many Guatemalan immigrants, especially the Maya, making a new home in the United States has not been easy. Many Maya people do not speak English or Spanish fluently. Because of the horror and trauma they experienced in the civil war, they often keep to themselves. At home, talking to the wrong person meant that you and your family could be killed.

Family

Many Guatemalan families in America work hard to adjust to their new life and to keep their ties with their Guatemalan heritage. For example, community centers organize traditional festivals that make Guatemalan immigrants feel at home in their new country. Although Spanish or Mayan languages are often spoken at home, parents know that their children's future depends upon their learning English. Keeping the family together and safe is very important in the Guatemalan culture. This hasn't been easy in recent years. Many families escaped the violence in their villages by moving to Mexico or to the United States. Life in America offers many opportunities to find work and support the family.

Work

Most Guatemalan immigrants in America work at low-paying jobs in the fields, at construction sites, or in factories. They are limited in the type of work they can find because of language difficulties and low levels of education. In addition, many Guatemalan immigrants entered the country illegally.

School

Many of the students from Guatemala arrive in the United States speaking some Spanish, but very little English. School districts that serve large populations of Guatemalan students, such as those in Los Angeles, California, and southern Florida, generally offer English as a second language or bilingual programs in Spanish.

One side effect of Guatemala's civil war was the destruction of much of the school system in rural areas. Children arrive in the United States farther behind in their studies than their American classmates. They must struggle to catch up, which can cause them to feel pressure and unhappiness. Although it isn't easy for them, immigrants who settle in areas with a large Guatemalan population can find support services through local churches and programs developed for their needs.

Religion

In America, Guatemalans are free to practice the religion of their choice. This is new and surprising for them. When Spanish conquerors arrived in Guatemala, they outlawed the Mayan religions and made Roman Catholicism the official religion. Many Maya continued to practice their religion in secret. Others combined their traditional beliefs with Catholic and Christian practices.

The traditional religion of the Maya people centers on the gods that rule their daily world. These include the rain god and the corn god. The study of astrology grew from the belief that the gods controlled everything that happened every day. By studying the sun, moon, and planets, the Maya could determine which days were best for planting or war.

Now Guatemalan immigrants practice a variety of religions. Most American communities offer many places to worship. The desire of many immigrants to stay in touch with their past and continue their family's rituals has resulted in a resurgence of their traditional religions.

During the civil war, a group called Catholic Action was active in Guatemala. The military believed that Catholic Action was encouraging the guerrillas. Soldiers tortured and killed people whom they believed were part of Catholic Action. Because of this persecution, many people converted to Protestant evangelical religions that were supported by the government.

Holidays and Festivals

Guatemalans have rich traditions associated with their religious holidays. However, the ongoing civil war has meant that holidays have been quiet affairs in recent years if they have been celebrated at all.

Each village in Guatemala has a patron saint who looks after it. The village usually has a festival honoring that saint each year. Guatemalan immigrants sometimes organize similar festivals in the United States. In southern Florida, for example, San Miguel Day is celebrated in September. Traditional music is played on the marimba. Songs and skits help Guatemalans remember their homeland.

Music

People throughout Guatemala enjoy marimba music. The marimba is a large instrument that looks like a xylophone. Usually two or three people play the marimba. Marimba orchestras, groups that include marimbas, trumpets, saxophones, banjos, and other percussion instruments, play during festivals. Large towns usually have their own marimba orchestra. Traveling groups provide music for smaller villages.

Maya priestesses prepare the altar for the new year ceremony at Kojba'l, a sacred site near Guatemala City. The Mayan calendar has a 260-day year.

Music in the cities is influenced by music from Mexico and from the United States.

Food

Guatemalan immigrants in the United States can usually find most of the ingredients they need to prepare their traditional dishes. A typical Ladino family eats both traditional foods and foods that are influenced by European and American trends. Pork and beef are popular for those who can afford them. Wheat bread often replaces tortillas.

The food eaten in Guatemala varies somewhat based on ethnic group and location. A traditional meal for native people includes corn tortillas, beans, and rice. Fruits such as bananas and plantains are eaten at many meals. Chicken is added to the meal on special occasions. Villagers generally grow their own food.

Recipe

Estofado de Chile Verde (Green Chili Stew)

2 pounds of pork, cut in pieces

4 cups of chicken broth

2 cans (14 ounces) of canned jalapeño peppers, cut into slices

2 pounds of tomatoes, washed and quartered

1 onion, finely chopped

1 clove of garlic, finely chopped

2 tablespoons of green chili powder

Heat a soup pot over medium-high heat. Add the pork meat, letting it cook in its own juices. Be careful not to overcook it. Add the remaining ingredients. Stir until thoroughly mixed.

Bring to a boil, stirring often. Reduce heat and simmer over low heat for at least two hours. Serve as a stew or as a topping for burritos.

Notes: For an improved flavor, cook the stew a day in advance and leave in the refrigerator overnight. This is a spicy dish. You may make it milder by using fewer jalapeño peppers or by substituting a mild green chili, such as *anaheim* or *poblano*.

Serves 8 to 10.

Source: Adapted from Lidia Peñate's Estofado de Chile Verde *(www.mayaparadise.com/recipeshow.asp?ID=18)*

CHAPTER SIX

Guyanese

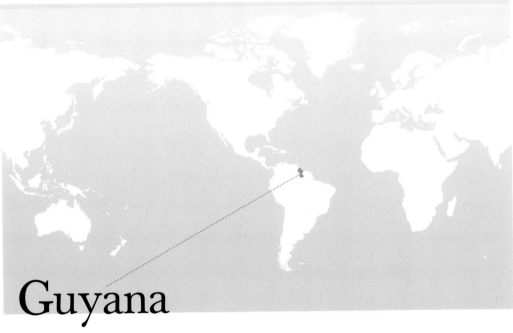

Guyana

is a unique country in South America. People speak English, rather than Spanish or Portuguese. It is considered part of the West Indies as well as South America. And most of the people who live there are *descendants* of East Indians (people from India).

Guyana is sometimes called the Land of Six Peoples. This name refers to the ethnic groups that have settled in the country: East Indian (Indo-Guyanese), African (Afro-Guyanese), Amerindian (native people, so called to distinguish them from Guyanese of East Indian descent), Chinese, Portuguese, and British. In addition to these six groups, there is a large population that has mixed ethnic backgrounds.

Although Guyana has had a relatively peaceful history compared to other South American countries, there has been discrimination and distrust between the different ethnic groups at different points in time. The main political parties are divided by race. The economy has been weak, making it hard for many families to make enough money to live on. These problems have led more and more people to immigrate to the United States.

The People of Guyana

a	East Indian	49%
b	African	32%
c	Mixed Race	12%
d	Amerindian	6%
e	European & Chinese	2%

Source: CIA World Factbook, *2002*

A Quick Look Back

In its earliest days, Guyana's *Amerindians* lived in a region that stretched from the Caribbean coast into the rain forest of South America. The many rivers found here gave the area its name–Guyana, Land of Many Waters. For centuries, no one but the Amerindians knew about this tropical land. Then the European explorers came to the region searching for land and riches.

The Europeans Arrive

It was about a century after Christopher Columbus's arrival in the New World that Europeans began exploring Guyana. The first to arrive was probably the English explorer Sir Walter Raleigh and his crew. Raleigh's search for El Dorado, the legendary city of gold, led him through the region in 1595.

The Dutch West Indian Company arrived from Holland in 1615. The Dutch established farms that later grew into plantations. The Dutch stopped Spanish ships carrying African slaves as they passed along the coast of Guyana and took the slaves back to their farms.

During this same time period, British and French planters began to settle in the region. They built sugar plantations that needed slaves too. By the late 1700s, the British, Dutch, and French all claimed to own Guyana. Control changed hands several times. The three countries finally divided the region into British Guiana, French Guiana, and Suriname (Dutch).

By now there were over 100,000 slaves in British Guiana and only a few hundred colonists. The slaves were not treated well. Revolts against the slave owners were common, with many lives being lost on both sides. One slave leader, Cuffy, became a national hero because of his fight for independence. Slavery finally ended in 1834.

Did you know?

The slave revolt in Haiti and the American and French Revolutions inspired slaves in British Guiana to fight for their own freedom.

A Changing Country

After slavery ended, most of the former slaves refused to work on the plantations anymore, even for wages. They migrated to urban areas and established themselves as professionals. To replace them, the planters invited immigrants from Europe,

China, and India to come to British Guiana as *indentured laborers*. The planters paid the travel expenses for the immigrants. In return, the indentured laborers agreed to work for a certain number of years on the sugar plantations. They were paid a small wage for their work. At the end of their agreement, the immigrants could stay in Guiana or return to their country. Today's population reflects the number of immigrants who came to Guyana from different countries during these years.

The British government appointed most of the colony's leaders throughout the 1800s and early 1900s, although colonists could elect a few representatives. Increased unrest in their colonies across the Caribbean region in the 1920s and 1930s convinced the British government to allow colonists more representation in their government. It wasn't until after World War II that the changes were implemented, though. In 1953, Guyana was given a new *constitution,* giving voting rights to all adults. Although Guyana remained a colony, it was allowed to select all its government representatives for the first time.

Self-Rule

The People's Progressive Party (PPP) was one of the first political parties in Guyana. It was led by Cheddi Jagan, an Indo-Guyanese, and Forbes Burnham, an Afro-Guyanese. They believed that British Guiana should be independent from Britain. The PPP advocated a *socialist* government that would own all the property and businesses. Workers would be paid equally based on the work they did.

When Jagan was elected as leader of Guyana in 1953, his views made the British government nervous. They removed him from office after only a few months. Then they appointed government leaders for the colony.

A few years later, the leaders of the PPP had a disagreement. Burnham left and started another party—the People's National Congress (PNC)—which represented the primarily Afro-Guyanese population in cities and towns. The PPP represented the rural Guyanese, who were mostly of East Indian descent. This split along racial lines still affects Guyana today.

In 1961, British Guiana gained full self-government, although it was still a British colony. When the PPP won a majority in the legislative elections that year, their leader, Cheddi Jagan, became the leader of Guyana again. Once in office, Jagan implemented unpopular economic policies.

People held strikes to protest. The Afro-Guyanese worried that the Indo-Guyanese had too much power. Several riots broke out in the cities during the early 1960s.

Dr. Cheddi Jagan attends a victory parade in Georgetown in 1961 following his victory in the general elections prior to Guyana's independence from Great Britain in 1966.

Independence

In 1964, neither party gained a legislative majority in the elections, so Britain appointed Burnham, head of the PNC, to lead Guyana. In this role, he led the movement for complete independence from Great Britain. On May 26, 1966, Britain declared that Guyana was an independent nation. Burnham was elected prime minister of the new country, which adopted cooperative socialism as its form of government. The government took over many businesses owned by foreign countries. It also set up relationships with Communist countries like China.

The new country did not do well economically during this time. Many people could not make a living. They left the country seeking better opportunities. Since most who left were educated, skilled workers, their departure caused even more

Brain Drain

When conditions in a country deteriorate, economically or politically, educated and skilled people are often the first to emigrate to other countries. This is described as a "brain drain." These creative, experienced people would normally be starting businesses, educating others, and pushing for change in government policies. With their departure, the remaining population often lacks the power or leadership to demand better government.

problems. By the end of the 1980s, Guyana had become one of the poorest nations in the Western world.

Burnham became increasingly dictatorial through the 1970s. He was reelected to the presidency several times, but Guyanese and international observers agreed that the elections were rigged to ensure Burnham's reelection. In 1980, Burnham oversaw changes in the constitution, one of which changed his title to executive president. Upon Burnham's death in 1985, his vice president, Hugh Desmond, became president. During his seven-year term, Desmond moved Guyana to a market economy that offered more opportunity for economic growth. He also restored freedom of the press and assembly.

Guyana Today

Since gaining independence in 1966, Guyana had been ruled by the primarily Afro-Guyanese PNC. This changed when the Indo-Guyanese-controlled PPP won the 1992 elections, widely recognized as the first fair elections held in Guyana. The PPP's leader, Cheddi Jagan, became president once again. Jagan continued the push to make Guyana more democratic. During his term, an expanding economy provided more jobs and higher incomes for most Guyanese.

When Jagan died in 1997, a special presidential election was held. Jagan's American-born wife, Janet Jagan, won the election, but the PNC charged that the election was not honest. A group of people from other countries investigated and did not find anything wrong with the elections. But the suspicions continued. The economy slowed down once again, causing hardship for many people.

Guyana's current president, Bharrat Jagdeo, took office in 1999 when Janet Jagan resigned due to health problems. He remained in office after winning the 2001 election. His presidency has been marked by many violent conflicts between the Afro- and Indo-Guyanese.

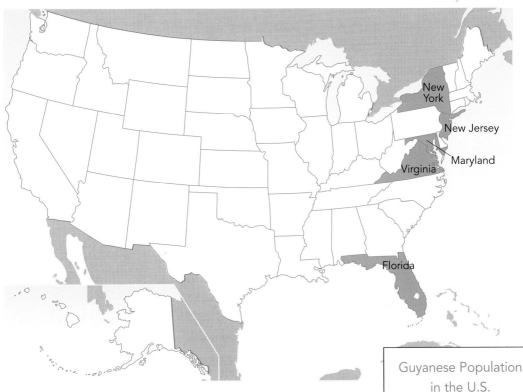

New York

New Jersey

Maryland

Virginia

Florida

Coming to America

Guyanese Population in the U.S.	
New York	78,529
New Jersey	15,771
Florida	7,136
Maryland	2,836
Virginia	2,119
Source: U.S. Census, 2000	

B efore 1965, few immigrants to the United States came from Guyana. As the U.S. immigration laws changed, Guyanese began moving to the United States in larger numbers. Nearly all of the immigrants who come to the United States are looking for better job opportunities. In the past twenty years, immigrants have also left their homes because of problems between the political groups in Guyana.

In 1996, Guyana was one of the top five countries sending immigrants to New York City. About five percent of New York City's immigrants that year came from Guyana. Since that time, the number of Guyanese immigrants to the United States has declined slightly.

Nearly all of the 5,746 Guyanese immigrants who entered the United States in 2000 came to rejoin their families. About 300 were admitted

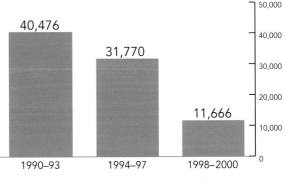

U.S./Guyanese Immigration by Years

40,476

31,770

11,666

1990–93   1994–97   1998–2000

50,000
40,000
30,000
20,000
10,000
0

Source: Statistical Yearbook of the Immigration and Naturalization Service

under the employment program for skilled and professional workers. Although Guyana is eligible for the *diversity lottery*, only a few immigrants come to the United States through that program.

Fast Facts

• Guyana is located in South America, but it is considered a country of the West Indies, or Caribbean. All other West Indian countries are islands. (When Christopher Columbus sighted the islands of the Caribbean in the late 1400s, he thought they were the western-most islands of the Indies—India and Southeast Asia—and dubbed them the West Indies.)

• Guyana is the only country in South America whose official language is English.

• About half of the people who live in Guyana are East Indians.

• The largest open-pit gold mine in South America is in Guyana.

The Rio Carroa Falls form a spectacular display along the border between Guyana and Venezuela.

Life in America

The Guyanese who immigrate to America have an advantage over many other immigrants. They come from a country where English is the official language. Most are literate—that is, they know how to read and write. And the two countries share a tradition of religious freedom for everyone.

There are some cultural adjustments, however. Immigrants may face racial or religious discrimination, especially the Afro-Guyanese and Muslims.

Family

Over the years, Guyanese immigrant families have worked to maintain their traditions. Their communities, in urban areas such as New York City and Washington, D.C., organize picnics and dances. They create newsletters to share news from home and information about adapting to the American culture. Many have also started charities that provide money and clothes to people in need in Guyana.

Work

Guyanese immigrants have two advantages in the U.S. workplace. They speak English and most are educated. They find work in all fields, including business, education, medicine, and industry. Many immigrants start their own businesses in America. Some sell items from Guyana, such as foods, videos, and clothes. Other businesses, including restaurants, jewelry stores, and courier services, reach out to the broader community.

Spotlight on
RAY RAFEEK

Ray Rafeek's $10 million business started with a $3,500 van and a drive around Queens, New York. Rafeek worked as a courier when he first arrived in the United States from Guyana. Couriers take important papers and packages from one place to another as quickly as possible. They have to know their way around the city where they work.

After a few years, friends encouraged Rafeek to start his own courier business. Rafeek planned carefully. In 1991, he and a partner opened 24 Hour Courier Service. The first day they made two deliveries.

The Guyana Connection

Nearly half a million people living in New York City have relatives in Guyana. Many travel between Guyana and New York City several times a year. Two Guyanese American sisters have made the trip easier (and less expensive) by opening their own airline—Universal Airlines.

Chandramatie Harpaul and Ramashree Singh worked with investors to get the airline started. It is based in Richmond Hill, Queens, home to most of the Guyanese who live in New York City.

The company leases an airplane from a Polish airline. It flies between Guyana and New York City four times a week carrying passengers, cargo, and mail.

The airline was set up with the needs of the immigrant community in mind. The flights leave at midnight, allowing travelers to complete their workday before flying to Guyana. Most Guyanese take gifts such as computers and clothes to their family in Guyana. The airline allows each passenger to take such baggage without paying extra fees.

Then Rafeek talked to other businesses. He convinced them that he could deliver their packages better than anyone else. The business started to grow. By 1998, Rafeek's company was making about 1,000 deliveries a day.

Rafeek has been active in the business community. In 1995, he was one of the people who participated in the White House Conference on Small Business. It was one of Rafeek's proudest moments.

School

Schools in Guyana are very much like schools in the United States. Children start school when they are five years old. They attend school five hours a day. And students in the two countries study many of the same subjects.

The biggest adjustment that students from Guyana have in the United States is often the language. Although English is the official language of Guyana, it is British English. The words and pronunciation are often quite different from American English. Even though they learn American English fairly quickly, Guyanese children often continue to use Guyanese English or Creole at home. Guyanese *Creole,* or *Creolese,* mixes English words and grammar with those of other languages.

Many schools have groups such as the Caribbean Culture Club. These groups encourage students to develop pride in their language and their culture.

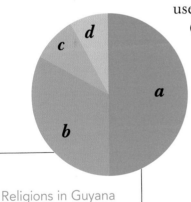

Religions in Guyana

a	Christians	50%
b	Hindu	33%
c	Muslim	9%
d	Other	8%

Source: CIA
World Factbook, *2002*

Religion

Little changes in Guyanese immigrants' religious practices when they arrive in America. Religious freedom is guaranteed in Guyana just as it is in the United States. Christians, Hindus, and Muslims all practice their religion freely in both countries. The different religions are somewhat divided by race. Nearly all of the Afro-Guyanese, Europeans, and Chinese are Christians. Most of the Indo-Guyanese are Hindu, with a small population of Muslims.

Holidays and Festivals

As each new ethnic group settled in Guyana, it brought along its own unique customs and holidays. Like their *ancestors,* Guyanese immigrants have brought their customs with them to the United States.

Christian Holidays

Easter, the celebration of the resurrection of Jesus Christ, is the most important Christian holiday of the year. Guyana and the United States share many of the same Easter customs. In Guyana, though, Easter is a national holiday. All businesses are closed the Friday before Easter. People spend this day thinking about Easter and what it means in their lives. Holy Week ends on the Monday after Easter, when people gather for daylong picnics and kite-flying.

Another important Christian holiday is Christmas, which celebrates Christ's birth. Guyanese families in both countries prepare for the holiday by cleaning and decorating the house, inside and out. Shopping centers are decorated. Christmas music is heard everywhere. In Guyana, families butcher a sheep, goat, chicken, or duck on Christmas morning. In the United States, however, they purchase fresh meat from the butcher's the week before since everyone is busy on Christmas morning.

Although Hindus and Muslims do not celebrate the Christmas holiday itself, they generally consider it part of the holiday season that follows their own celebrations of Eid al-Fitr and Diwali. Families often mark the day with a special meal.

Hindu Celebrations

The Hindu holiday of Phagwah (FOG-wah), or Holi, is a spring celebration of good winning over evil. In Guyana, all the businesses close for the holiday. People wear white clothing. They buy a red dye called *abeer,* which represents the blood of a cruel king who was killed for making his people suffer so much. During parades, people throw the red dye on each other. They may also throw powder or spray each other with water. Both Hindus and non-Hindus have fun with this holiday.

In the United States, Hindus continue to celebrate Phagwah. Some changes have been made, though. If the holiday falls during the workweek, Phagwah is celebrated the weekend before or after the actual day. People continue to splash each other with red dye and water, but it is much colder in New York in the spring! Celebrations at the temples are followed by parades. In the United States, the holiday ends with a concert. One thing does not change: the holiday brings all Guyanese together, without regard for religion or race.

Another Hindu festival that is celebrated in Guyanese communities in the United States is Diwali, the festival of lights. Diwali, celebrated in mid-November, is a time for joy and happiness. It is also a time when Guyanese take up donations of food, money, and clothing for those in need.

In Guyana, Diwali is a national holiday and no one has to work. In America, the celebrations are generally held after work. The celebration of Diwali in the United States is much more extravagant than in Guyana. People decorate their homes and businesses with big light displays and with *diyas* (small lamps). The lights often stay up through the Christmas season. Friends and family members visit and exchange gifts and greetings. Most of the visiting occurs indoors, though, due to New York's colder weather.

Muslim Holidays

Ramadan is the most important month in the Islamic year and is observed by Guyanese immigrants throughout the United States. It is called the month of blessing. Muslims do not eat or drink from dawn until dusk during Ramadan. Prayer and works of charity are also important parts of this holiday.

As Ramadan ends, Muslims gather with family and friends to celebrate the feast of Eid al-Fitr. Children often get new clothes for the holiday, which usually lasts about three days.

Other Celebrations

Carnival is celebrated in most Caribbean and South American countries. It is held just before the Christian season of Lent begins in the spring. Many U.S. cities hold Carnival parades and parties. Musicians and costumed dancers from many different Caribbean countries, including Guyana, join together to celebrate Carnival.

Anslem Douglas, a soca musician, wrote the song "Who Let the Dogs Out," which is often played at baseball and football games in the United States.

Music

Guyanese music blends the rhythms and sounds of the Caribbean with other musical forms. "Soca" and "chutney" music were born in Guyana, Trinidad, and other West Indian countries. Soca, short for soul of calypso, blends calypso with American rhythm and blues. Chutney music mixes Indian music and words with calypso and soca.

The indentured workers from India brought their folk music with them. The songs were religious, but had a strong beat that made people want to dance. In the 1970s, musicians released new songs that weren't religious. Western instruments like the guitar were added. This new mix was called chutney music after the hot, spicy Indian food. It went through several changes over the next twenty years. Calypso rhythms were added. Afro-Guyanese musicians began recording the music. It found large audiences in the United States and Canada in the 1980s. Most recently, chutney music has become more traditional. The words of the songs are in Hindi, even though few Guyanese Americans speak the language well. This latest version is called chutney soca. For many young people, both from India and the Caribbean, it has become a link to their culture and traditions.

Food

The food of Guyana reflects the many backgrounds of its people. Flavors and ingredients from the Caribbean, India, Africa, China, Portugal, Britain, and Holland combine with the native Amerindian food to make truly unique dishes. Pepperpot stew, Indian curries and roti, British pastries, and Chinese noodle dishes are considered classic Guyanese foods.

Peanut and Banana Punch

2 1/2 cups milk

5 tablespoons condensed milk

1/2 banana

3 tablespoons smooth natural peanut butter

1/4 teaspoon cinnamon

1/4 teaspoon vanilla

a little crushed ice

Put all the ingredients in a blender. Blend on low until ice begins to break apart, then blend on high until drink is slushy. Serve immediately.

Makes 3 servings.

Source: Adapted from Caribbean and African Cooking by Rosamund Grant

CHAPTER SEVEN

Haitians

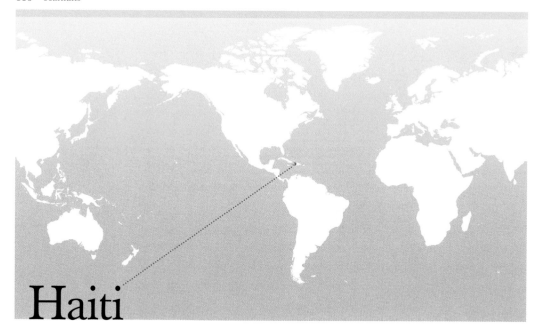

Haiti

is a small country lying in the Caribbean Sea, 600 miles (960 kilometers) southeast of Florida. This mountainous country has a proud heritage. Nearly 200 years ago, Haiti became the first independent black nation in the Western Hemisphere.

The ties between the United States and Haiti go back over two centuries. About 800 Haitians fought in the American Revolution under General Lafayette. American companies have opened factories in Haiti. American troops have also been sent to Haiti, sometimes against the wishes of the Haitian people.

The need to escape from a harsh government and the dream of a better life has led many Haitians to try to reach the United States. In recent years, this has often meant selling everything they own. Then they pay for passage on boats that were never intended for the rough seas between Haiti and America. The passengers may not have enough food and water to last for the entire trip. The boat may leak badly or fall apart at sea. It is estimated that hundreds of Haitians have drowned trying to get to the United States. Most of those who do make it to the United States without a visa have been returned to Haiti.

Today, over a million Haitians and Haitian Americans live in the United States. Most settle in Florida and the New York City area. They make up one of the largest groups of immigrants, both legal and illegal, from the Caribbean region.

A Quick Look Back

Haiti's history is one of rebellion and war. It is often a story of the strong ruling the weak and powerless. But, more importantly, it is the story of proud people stepping forward to claim power for themselves.

The Europeans Arrive

In 1492, Christopher Columbus set out from Spain to find a new trade route to the East Indies, the area now known as India and Southeast Asia. When land was sighted, Columbus declared that he had discovered the westernmost islands of the Indies and named the area the West Indies. This name is still used to describe the group of islands in the Caribbean Sea. As Columbus made his way through the islands, his boat hit a reef near the island he called Hispaniola. The sailors made it ashore and were greeted by the native people, whom Columbus called Indians. When the boat was fixed, the sailors continued exploring the islands.

A year later, Columbus returned to Hispaniola. He started the first permanent European settlement, located in what is now the Dominican Republic. The Spanish colonists were anxious to find gold. They made slaves of the Indians and forced them to dig in the mines. The Indians had to work very hard, but they were not given much to eat. Many of the Indians died from working too hard. Others starved to death. The diseases brought by the Spanish settlers also killed many Indians. In less than sixty years, the Indian people had been wiped out. The Spanish turned to West Africa for slaves to replace the Indian laborers.

> **Did you know?**
>
> The native people in the West Indies crushed the red seed from the annatto plant and rubbed the powder on their bodies to repel insects. Columbus, seeing this for the first time, referred to them as "redskins."

The Spanish settlers focused on the eastern part of the island, leaving the western coast unguarded. French colonists began settling in the western regions of Hispaniola. In 1697, Spain and France agreed that France would own the western one-third of the island. The French called their colony St. Domingue.

The French built large farms, or plantations, on St. Domingue. It took a lot of people to build a plantation and to plant and harvest the crops. The French followed the lead of Spain, forcing the Indians to work on the plantations. As they died from overwork and diseases, the French also began using slaves from Africa. By 1789, about 1 million slaves had been brought to the colony.

Over the next hundred years, the French colony became one of the richest in the world. The sugar, coffee, cocoa, and indigo that it produced on the plantations were highly prized in Europe. The slaves who worked on the plantations were treated just as badly as the Indians had been. Beatings were frequent. They often died of starvation and overwork.

At the end of the eighteenth century, there were about fifteen slaves for every French colonist. There were also significant numbers of mulattoes. These were people of both African and European descent. Most of the mulattoes were free, but they did not have as many rights as the white settlers.

Around the world, people were starting to fight for their freedom and independence. American colonists won their independence from Britain in the Revolutionary War (1776–1783). A few years later, in 1789, the French Revolution began. The news of the two revolutions inspired the slaves in St. Domingue.

A New Country is Born

The slaves in the northern region began making plans in secret. In 1791, led by Toussaint L'Ouverture (TOO-sant LOO-vair-tour), they began to fight for their independence. The slaves killed the French colonists and burned everything on the plantations. Houses, buildings, crops, and irrigation systems were all destroyed. As the fight for independence spread to other parts of the colony, the mulattoes joined in the revolt. Over the next few years, the former slaves drove out or killed the remaining colonists. They defeated the armies sent by France, Spain, and England.

Thirteen years after the original revolt, in 1804, the former slaves and the mulattoes declared their independence from France. The new country was called Haiti. It became the first free black nation in the New World.

Building a Nation

The years after the revolution were difficult. The destruction of the plantations helped drive out the colonists, but it left the new country in bad shape. Friendship with France prevented countries around the world from helping Haiti. Other countries, such as the United States, didn't get involved because they thought it would encourage their own slaves to rebel.

Just before independence was declared, L'Ouverture created a dictatorship, a form of government in which one person holds most of the power and makes all the decisions. The military was given the power to make sure people followed the laws along with special privileges for supporting the government. From the start, those without military ties had few rights.

A program forcing the former slaves to resume farming was put into place. Some money started coming in as crops were sold, but ongoing power struggles between the mulattoes and the former slaves caused chaos. One leader after another was killed or forced out of office by the military.

The United States grew increasingly concerned about the instability in Haiti in the early 1900s. A small community of Germans living in Haiti controlled some utilities and transportation services, as well as most of Haiti's international business. U.S. foreign policy at the time was focused on preventing European interference with countries in the Western Hemisphere. When World War I broke out in Europe, the United States worried that Germany might try to take over the unstable government in Haiti and use it as a base to attack the United States. To prevent this, the U.S. Marines were sent to Haiti to restore order.

Because there was no clear plan for what the United States wanted to accomplish in Haiti, the occupation lasted twenty years. During this time, the United States paid for many

Shown here with sword and paper in hand, Toussaint L'Ouverture was the key figure in the liberation of Haiti from France in 1801.

improvements in roads, schools, and health care. It set up a school for the military. It also took control of the national bank, collecting taxes and paying off Haiti's foreign debt.

Although these changes were positive, Haitians resented the U.S. presence. The occupying troops held deep racial prejudices, which resulted in the use of forced labor in construction and the imposition of a new constitution that favored U.S. business interests. For the first time since 1804, foreigners were allowed to own property and land in Haiti.

In the early 1930s, Haitians began to demand an end to the American occupation. U.S. troops were finally withdrawn in 1934. Within a few years, political instability returned to Haiti.

The Duvaliers

François Duvalier (DOO-val-yea) was a well-respected doctor in Haiti. People called him "Papa Doc" as a sign of his fatherly role in their lives. He was also a member of the Griots, a group of black intellectuals who opposed Haiti's elite made up mostly of mulattoes. When he decided to run for president, he promised to give the people of Haiti more power in their government. Behind the scenes, though, Duvalier worked with the military to make sure that he won the election. Many people were taken to the polls by armed soldiers and told to vote for Duvalier, who became president in 1957.

Once in office, Papa Doc consolidated his power and soon became one of the cruelest dictators ever to rule over Haiti. It is estimated that 30,000 people were killed for political reasons during his fourteen years in office, many of them mulattoes.

After an attempted coup in 1958, Duvalier put together a group of armed men called the Tonton Macoutes. They obeyed Papa Doc absolutely, beating or killing anyone who was declared to be an enemy. In return, Papa Doc gave them the power to do anything they wanted. They terrorized people in villages, accusing them of criticizing Duvalier. They often declared a tax on villagers and kept the money for themselves. The Tonton Macoutes were not punished for any crimes they committed. As Papa Doc grew more powerful, many middle-class Haitians left the country. A number of them settled in the United States.

Papa Doc's government was very corrupt. Much of the foreign-aid money, which was supposed to be used to improve the country, was deposited directly into the bank accounts of Papa Doc and his friends. When the United States withheld

Did you know?

The Tonton Macoutes were named after a bogeyman from Creole myths.

aid from Haiti, Duvalier suggested that he would turn to the Communists for help instead. By 1963, the United States had reluctantly accepted Duvalier's presidency, although it didn't resume sending aid until 1971.

Papa Doc declared himself "president for life" and claimed the right to choose his successor. He announced that his son, Jean-Claude Duvalier, known as Baby Doc, would become the president of Haiti after his death.

General Antonio Kebreau pins a medal on François Duvalier during the inauguration ceremony following Papa Doc's election as president of Haiti in 1957.

Baby Doc was nineteen years old when he became president in 1971. In the early years of his presidency, his mother controlled most of the government functions. Gradually, though, Duvalier assumed more power. He relaxed some of the repressive programs instituted by his father, including some mulattoes in his government and allowing more freedom of speech. While

Baby Doc wasn't as cruel as his father, he did continue to use the Tonton Macoutes to enforce his rules. He also used the national treasury as his own personal bank account. He lived a luxurious life while millions of Haitians struggled to grow or buy enough food to stay alive. When he married a mulatto woman in 1980, he spent millions of dollars on the wedding. This expense, combined with his wife's luxurious and irresponsible lifestyle, made Haitians furious. Millions of Haitians, including the black middle class that had supported his father, protested his presidency. Under pressure from the United States and the Haitian military, Jean-Claude Duvalier and his wife fled the country for France in 1986.

Former Haitian president Jean-Bertrand Aristide celebrates the second anniversary of his return to Haiti in 1994 following three years of exile. More than 300 children from an orphanage he sponsors attended the ceremony.

The Move to Democracy

After Baby Doc left the country, the army took over the government for five years. A new constitution was written and approved, and an election was scheduled for 1990.

Jean-Bertrand Aristide (A-ri-steed) was a popular Roman Catholic priest who had worked with Haiti's poor for years. He had spoken out against Baby Doc's government despite threats against his life. A few months before the election, Aristide announced that he would run for president. With excited Haitians supporting his campaign, he was elected president by a wide margin.

Once in office, Aristide began proposing changes. He wanted businesses to pay people more money for the work they did. He talked about breaking up the army and keeping only a small force. He also described new programs for schools. The poor people of Haiti were filled with hopes of a better life. The changes made wealthy business owners and the military leaders very nervous, though. Raoul Cédras (SAY-drah), an army lieutenant, led a coup against Aristide before he had completed his first year as president. Because of his popularity, Aristide wasn't killed. He was allowed to leave the country, traveling to Venezuela first and later settling in the United States.

Countries around the world were outraged that a freely elected president had been removed from office. They insisted that the army return Aristide to the presidency. When Cédras didn't cooperate, the United Nations (UN) imposed economic sanctions. Only food and medicine could be sent to Haiti; gasoline, oil, and other goods could not be sold to Haiti by UN members. These actions hurt the poor people of Haiti much more than the wealthy who had backed the takeover; they could afford to buy fuel and other goods that were smuggled into Haiti from the Dominican Republic.

Finally, in 1994, with a threat of invasion by the United States, Cédras gave up power. The UN and U.S. forces took control of Haiti's capital, Port-au-Prince. Jean-Bertrand Aristide then returned to Haiti and continued his presidency.

Aristide was not able to make many changes with only two years left in his term. He was elected president again in 2000, although few people voted. Many people in the international community believe that the elections were poorly organized, and there were concerns about how the votes were counted. They are waiting to see if Aristide can make changes that will really bring equality and justice to Haiti.

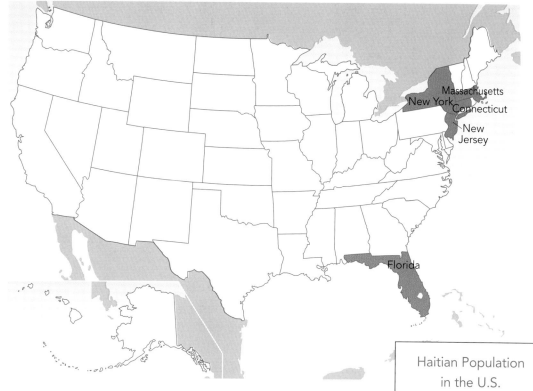

Haitian Population in the U.S.	
Florida	266,284
New York	181,603
Massachusetts	46,343
New Jersey	43,014
Connecticut	22,540

Source: U.S. Census, 2000

Coming to America

Haitian immigrants and refugees attempting to enter the United States in the past twenty-five years have met with much resistance. Coming from one of the Western Hemisphere's poorest and least developed countries, they are often assumed to be immigrating for economic reasons. This assumption has led to a policy of stopping Haitians before they reach America and returning them to their homes. In the 1980s, only six Haitians were allowed to enter the U.S. to claim asylum. From 1989 through 1996, only 8.4 percent of Haitians who applied for asylum were allowed to come to the United States. In contrast, people leaving the neighboring island of Cuba have long been assumed to be political refugees. They are

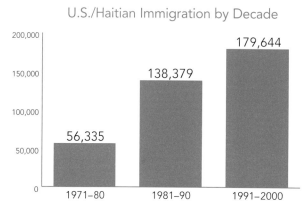

U.S./Haitian Immigration by Decade

1971–80	1981–90	1991–2000
56,335	138,379	179,644

Source: Statistical Yearbook of the Immigration and Naturalization Service

allowed to enter the United States, and those who are granted asylum (nearly all) receive *resettlement* benefits that help them establish a new life. This difference in policy has led to charges of racial discrimination: Haitians are black; most Cubans are not.

The first wave of Haitian immigrants arrived in the late 1950s and early 1960s. These mostly middle-class, educated immigrants were fleeing the dictatorship of François Duvalier. Many were teachers, doctors, engineers, or other professionals. Most of these immigrants chose to settle in the New York City area due to the racism against blacks that was more prevalent in the southern United States. They established a settlement pattern for one of the largest Haitian communities in the United States today.

In the late 1970s and 1980s, in response to increasingly desperate political and economic conditions, a second wave of Haitians began making their way to America. This time, they crowded onto boats and set off for southern Florida. By 1986, tens of thousands of people were leaving Haiti each year. In contrast to the earlier Haitian immigrants, this second wave had little education. Three decades of government neglect and corruption had virtually eliminated the opportunity for education for most Haitians.

The United States viewed the growing numbers of Haitians immigrants with concern. Such a large influx of people seeking asylum threatened to overwhelm the state of Florida. (The costs of resettlement benefits, including medical and social services, for refugees and *asylees* are paid by the state where they settle.) In addition, it was widely believed that most Haitians were seeking better economic opportunities, a reason no longer valid under new immigration laws, and thus would be classified as illegal immigrants.

President Ronald Reagan and other U.S. political leaders negotiated a deal with Haiti's leaders. The U.S. Coast Guard would stop Haitian boats when they reached American waters. Immigration and Naturalization Service (INS) officers would interview the Haitians on board the Coast Guard ships. Haitians who did not qualify as refugees would be returned to Haiti. Haiti agreed not to arrest the people who were sent back. During the 1980s, the United States stopped about 25,000 Haitians; only six were allowed to continue to the United States to apply for refugee status.

The third wave of Haitian immigrants poured out of Haiti in the early 1990s following the military coup that forced President Jean-Bertrand Aristide from office. The new military leaders launched a campaign to silence anyone who opposed them. Aristide's supporters were imprisoned, tortured, and—often—killed. Even Haitians who had not openly taken sides were afraid that they would be killed. Once again, those who could pay the price took to the seas.

The Coast Guard continued stopping Haitian boats at sea. The INS interviewed those aboard to determine if they met the conditions for political asylum. Because of the situation in Haiti, the United States debated what to do about those who did not qualify for asylum. In November 1991, President George H.W. Bush decided to return them to Haiti. Haitian American groups sued the U.S. government, claiming that the screening process used by the INS wasn't reliable enough to identify all refugees and protect them from a forced return to Haiti. (According to international law, refugees could not be forced to return to their country if they had a credible, or believable, fear of persecution because of their race, religion, or political opinion.)

The judge who heard the case ordered that no Haitians be returned. His ruling was appealed and overturned in February 1992. In the meantime, the United States set up a refugee camp at the U.S. Marine base at Guantánamo Bay, Cuba. By May 1992, the refugee camp was full. The U.S. government had to decide between letting Haitians enter America to file for asylum or send them back to Haiti. Presidential advisers argued that allowing the Haitians to enter the United States would slow down diplomatic efforts to restore Aristide to the presidency in Haiti. They also claimed that this option would encourage more Haitians to leave their country, making it even harder to protect American borders from illegal immigrants. The second choice, returning Haitians to their country to file for asylum, could endanger those who were true political refugees.

President Bush chose the second option and ordered that all Haitians trying to leave Haiti be returned to their country. They could then apply for asylum at INS centers that the United States would set up on Haiti. More lawsuits were filed, accusing the United States of not following international refugee law. One lawsuit claimed that Haitians who were taken aboard Coast Guard ships had, in effect, reached American shores. This would mean that Haitians could not be returned to Haiti until they had received an asylum hearing. The U.S. Supreme Court ruled in favor of the government in 1993, saying that the refugee laws applied only to those who physically entered the United States. The policy of stopping Haitians at sea and automatically returning them to Haiti continues today.

About half of the Haitians who live in the United States have settled in the New York City area. About half live in southern Florida, as well. Sizable communities are also found in Massachusetts and Connecticut. While a large number of Haitians are poor or working-class, there is a growing middle class. While hundreds of Haitians enter the United States through the employment-based preference programs each year, the vast majority enter through programs designed to reunite families that have been separated.

Spotlight on
EDWIDGE DANTICAT

Writer Edwidge Danticat at an interview in New York City in 1989.

Edwidge Danticat (pronounced Ed-*weedj* Dan-ti-*cah*) knows what it is like to move to a new country and live with parents who have become strangers. She remembers how painful it was not to fit in at school. Danticat weaves those feelings into her award-winning writing as she explores themes of identity, loss, and fitting into a different culture.

In a pattern that is typical for many immigrant families, Danticat's father left Haiti for New York when she was two years old. Her mother joined her husband two years later. Danticat stayed in Haiti with her aunt.

When she was twelve years old, her parents sent for her. After being apart from her parents for eight years, it took some time to get to know them again. Danticat started junior high school soon after her arrival. In an essay in *Becoming American,* Danticat tells of being teased about her clothing and her accent. Finally, she and the other Haitian students began carrying red handkerchiefs and spread rumors that the handkerchiefs were Voodoo objects. Whenever someone was mean to them, they pretended to put a spell on them. Soon, the teasing stopped.

Danticat's first book, *Breath, Eyes, Memory,* was written as part of her master's degree program at Brown University. Oprah Winfrey selected it as one of her Reading Club selections in 1998. Danticat's second book, *Krik? Krak!,* is a collection of short stories. The title comes from the Haitian story-telling tradition. After supper, someone calls out, "Krik?" asking for a story. Whoever has a story to tell replies, "Krak!" The book was a finalist for the National Book Award in 1995.

Danticat has written or edited several other books that have been widely praised, including a collection of essays by Haitians who are living in exile in the United States.

Fast Facts

• With 85 percent of the population living in poverty, Haiti is one of the poorest countries in the Western Hemisphere.

• Haiti is the first independent republic in the Western Hemisphere founded by blacks.

• Haitians are one of the largest groups of Caribbean immigrants in the United States.

Life in America

Haitian immigrants who arrived in the United States in the past twenty-five years have not had an easy adjustment. They were introduced to Americans through news reports about poor, black, uneducated "boat people" who were trying to reach the shores of the United States. The communities where they lived did not welcome them warmly. Instead, they were often the target of prejudice. The fact that they spoke French and Haitian *Creole,* a language that combines

French and African languages, limited their ability to communicate in the United States. It also limited their job opportunities.

When news stories in the 1980s said that many Haitians carried dangerous diseases, it became even harder to find work and fit in. The state of Florida identified Haitians as a public health threat. It said that many Haitians had tuberculosis, a very contagious lung disease, in addition to AIDS and other diseases. The health scares were later found to be false, but the damage had been done. Haitians were often regarded as outcasts in their communities.

Although Haitians have not been warmly welcomed in America, most are determined to make it their home. Research in Miami-Dade County in Florida shows that more Haitian immigrants own their own homes than any other immigrant group.

Family

Like most immigrants, Haitian families often have conflicts after their move to the United States. The reasons for these conflicts are many. Among the most common problems are language and discipline conflicts.

People from Haiti speak French and Creole. (Haitian Creole combines the words and sentence patterns of French with several different African languages.) Neither language is spoken much in the United States. This presents special difficulties for parents who do not speak English well. Many rely on their children to tell them what written notices say. The children often have to help their parents deal with businesses such as the gas or electric company.

Sometimes children get upset with this added responsibility. They think that their parents should learn English faster. They are often embarrassed that their parents speak or act so differently from their classmates' parents. As children and teenagers try to fit in at school, they lose fluency in their native Creole language. This makes it even harder to talk with their parents about issues that are important in their lives.

Two dancers from Shadowlawn Elementary School in the Little Haiti section of Miami, Florida, dance a traditional compas dance as part of the 2002 Miami Haitian Heritage Celebration.

The struggle for parents to remain in charge of the family is another big problem facing Haitian families. In Haiti, children know that parents can tell them how to act, even when they are adults. It is the parents' job to make sure children behave themselves. They can discipline children however they think best. In the United States, parents lose some of their power when their children learn English more quickly than they do. The children also learn that the United States has different family values. Parents often have less control over their children, especially adult children, than they do in Haiti.

With many Haitian families living in inner-city neighborhoods, children often see a way of life that parents do not want them to follow. There may be gangs or other negative influences that turn kids away from education and family life. Haitian parents typically place strict limits on their children. But, after being in America for a while, the children may start questioning their parents' right to make these decisions.

Physical discipline, such as hitting, is fairly common in Haiti. This practice is frowned upon in the United States. Haitian parents understand that their children can bring legal charges against them for physically punishing the children. Parents feel trapped. If they do not discipline their children, the children could end up in trouble with the police. If they do discipline their children, the parents risk punishment and disapproval from the greater community. Even though immigration can cause problems within families, Haitian children continue to place high importance on their family, according to studies of immigrant children.

Work

The first big wave of Haitian immigrants brought mostly educated, professional people to the United States. They found work as doctors, teachers, and engineers, as well as shopkeepers and cabdrivers. Today most are firmly established in their communities.

The immigrants and refugees who arrived in the 1980s and 1990s had more trouble entering the job market. Language differences and low levels of education meant that most would qualify only for the lowest-paying jobs if they could find work at all. As stories about high levels of tuberculosis and AIDS within the Haitian community spread, many employers refused to hire Haitians. The immigrants often started working independently, providing services such as child care or sewing. Some were hired by the day for construction work or yard work.

Today, Haitians can be found at every level of employment in the United States, from engineers and entertainers to maids and manual laborers. After several decades in the United States, Haitians are finding their political voice as well. Many are serving as judges and elected representatives of their cities and states.

School

Haitian students often face more obstacles in school than other immigrants. As a group, they are isolated from other students by their language—Haitian Creole, which is spoken nowhere but Haiti. Most of those who arrived in the past twenty years had little schooling in Haiti. They are also frequently the victims of discrimination, both as people of African heritage and as Haitians.

In the early 1980s, large numbers of Haitians began attending schools in Miami. Because of all the negative images in the news media at the time, most students and many adults looked down on the Haitians. Kids often used "Haitian" as a curse word. High schools often had to be closed for a short time due to fights on campus. Some Haitian students were beaten up. Others were the targets of mean jokes and teasing. Although things have improved somewhat over the years, there are still many stories of prejudice and exclusion.

A three-year study of the children of immigrants in Miami found that Haitian students lost the ability to speak Haitian Creole relatively quickly. Students reported learning English as soon as possible so that others couldn't identify them as Haitian. Some students in the study referred to themselves as African American rather than Haitian. The researchers felt this was a way to avoid the emotional pain that often goes along with being Haitian in America.

Religion

Religion in Haiti is often a combination of European and African traditions. The Spanish and French colonists brought the Roman Catholic religion to Haiti. Slaves from Africa brought their own religion, a colorful belief in different spirits, called Voodoo (sometimes called Vodun, Vodou, or Vodoun). While most Haitians are Roman Catholic, about half practice both religions.

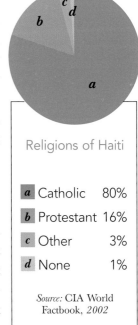

Religions of Haiti

a Catholic 80%

b Protestant 16%

c Other 3%

d None 1%

Source: CIA World Factbook, *2002*

Christianity

Christianity, particularly Roman Catholicism, is widespread in Haiti. Catholicism was introduced by the colonists from Spain and France. When they brought slaves from Africa, the slaves had to become Catholics. Until the 1970s, nearly everyone in Haiti was Catholic. Today, some Catholic churches in Haiti use Voodoo music during the mass as a way to honor the past.

Evangelical Christianity came to Haiti during the 1970s. Evangelical Christians, such as Baptists and Pentecostals, emphasize preaching to others in the community or in other nations about God and Jesus. Members explain their beliefs about salvation, or being saved from sin.

Haitian immigrants continue to worship in Roman Catholic and Protestant churches in the United States. Churches in areas that have large Haitian communities offer services in French and Creole. They may also offer help in adjusting to life in the United States, such as English lessons.

Wydef Jean of the musical group The Fugees sings at a concert for Haitian refugees expelled from the Dominican Republic in 1997. The group's name is short for "refugees."

Holidays and Festivals

Carnival is one of the biggest celebrations of the year for the nations in the West Indies. Held in the spring, Carnival gives people a chance to celebrate and have fun before the season of Lent begins. Parades, music, dancing, and food are all part of the Carnival celebration.

Many cities in the United States hold their own Carnival parades. Haitians and Haitian Americans join with people from other Caribbean backgrounds in Washington, D.C., Miami, and New York to celebrate this part of their heritage.

The Arts

Haiti produces a large number of artists, especially painters. While some have received formal training in Haiti or another country, most are self-taught.

Their work is featured in galleries across the United States and in other countries. Many Haitian American artists live in and around Miami, but Queens, New York, is home to the largest Haitian American artists' colony in America.

Music has always played an important role in Haitian life, in traditional religious ceremonies and in simple gatherings of friends and family. This is true in the United States as well as in Haiti. As Haitian musicians reach wider audiences, events like the Haitian Music Entertainment Awards ceremony celebrate the achievements of musicians and other stars.

Spotlight on
FRISNER AUGUSTIN

Music, especially drumming, and dancing are an important part of traditional Haitian life. Master drummer and teacher Frisner Augustin has spent the last twenty years introducing the music of his country to America.

As a child growing up in one of the poorest neighborhoods in Haiti's capital, Augustin knew he wanted to be a musician. Since drums cost only $2, much less than a trumpet or saxophone, he became a drummer. He learned quickly and was in great demand. By the age of seven, Augustin was playing drums at Carnival and in religious ceremonies. He joined a group that performed throughout the Caribbean, Latin America, and the United States.

After a show in New York City in the early 1970s, Augustin decided to stay in the United States. People asked him to perform at ceremonies. He also began teaching young people about the traditional music of Haiti. In 1999, Augustin was awarded a National Heritage Fellowship in the Folk and Traditional Arts by the National Endowment for the Arts for his contributions.

Food

In some U.S. communities, Haitian cooking classes are offered so young people can learn some of their cultural traditions.

Did you know?

Foods from home can be hard for new immigrants to find. *Djon-djon*, the dried black mushrooms used in Haitian cooking, is often sold on the street in New York's Haitian neighborhoods. The sellers rely on friends and family to bring the mushrooms back from trips to Haiti. *Djon-djon* is also found at many markets that sell foods from the West Indies.

The food of Haiti combines the flavors and traditions of Spain, France, and West Africa. Many different kinds of meats are found in dishes, including conch, pork, goat, and chicken. Rice is one of the main foods of Haiti. It is often made with beans or with dried black mushrooms called *djon-djon*. Plantains, sweet potatoes, pumpkins, and other vegetables round out the Haitian diet.

Djon-Djon (Haitian Rice)

2 to 3 tablespoons (1 ounce) *djon-djon* (any dried mushrooms, such as porcini or shiitake, may be substituted)

about 1 cup boiling water

1 ounce slab bacon, finely minced, or 2 tablespoons butter

3 green onions, including tops, chopped

1/2 green or red bell pepper, seeded and chopped

3 garlic cloves, minced

1/4 teaspoon dried thyme, crushed

1 1/2 cups long-grain white rice, rinsed and drained

2 cups water or chicken stock, heated

salt and ground black pepper

In a bowl, combine the mushrooms and enough boiling water to cover. Let stand 15 minutes until the caps have softened. Remove the mushrooms, then strain and reserve the soaking liquid. Chop the mushrooms. (If using dried shiitake mushrooms, cut off and discard the tough stems before chopping.) Set the mushrooms and liquid aside.

In a 10- or 12-inch skillet, fry the bacon over medium heat until crisp (or melt the butter). Add the green onions and bell pepper and sauté until just soft, about 1 minute. Stir in the garlic, thyme, and rice. Cook to coat the rice, about 1 minute. Stir in the hot water. Add the mushrooms and strained liquid and bring to a boil. Season with salt and pepper, reduce the heat to medium-low, cover, and cook until the liquid is absorbed and the rice is tender, 15 to 18 minutes.

When the rice is cooked, uncover and, using a fork, fluff the rice to evenly distribute the ingredients. Serve immediately.

Serves 6.

Source: Adapted from Soul and Spice: African Cooking in the Americas *by Heidi Haughy Cusick*

Glossary

Amerindian a word used to describe people who were the first to settle in the Americas, especially South America and the Caribbean (the term "Native American" is more commonly used in the United States)

ancestors people from whom a person is descended (great-grandparents, great-great-grandparents, etc.)

asylum protection; countries such as the United States sometimes grant asylum to people who are in danger of being killed or imprisoned for their political or religious beliefs

bilingual program an educational program that teaches students in two different languages, usually their own language and English

civilization a highly developed society that demonstrates progress in the arts and sciences, keeps some form of written records, and creates political and social organizations

civil war war among citizens of one country

colony people who inhabit a new territory, or the territory itself

Communist a person who supports Communism, a totalitarian government that controls the wealth or money in a country; there is only one political party and it holds all the power

conqueror a person who gains control of a country by force

constitution a paper that states what a country's laws are and how the people will be governed

coup (pronounced "koo") shortened version of coup d'état, the overthrow of a government, usually by a small group

Creole, Creolese a language that combines two or more languages, such as French or English and a traditional African language

descendant a person whose descent can be traced to a particular country or ethnic group

diversity lottery a drawing that awards extra visas to people from countries who have not sent a lot of immigrants to the United States in the past

drought long periods with little or no rain

dynasty a family of powerful leaders that is maintained over generations

economy how a country makes and spends money. In a strong economy, many people have jobs and can buy what they need. In a weak economy, people are often out of work and worry about whether they will be able to pay their bills.

exile having to live in another country because of political or religious reasons; a person who is forced to leave his or her country

genocide the murder of everyone in a specific national, ethnic, or religious group

guerrillas armed fighters, usually those who are trying to overthrow their government

immigrant a person who moves from one country to live in another

immigrate to come to a country with plans to live there

indentured laborers workers who agree to move to a new country and work for little or no pay for a certain number of years in exchange for travel expenses to the new country

indigenous people the first people to settle in a country or region; native people

inflation a continual rise in prices

nativist person or group who opposes the presence of immigrants or foreigners in the United States

naturalized citizen someone born in a country other than the United States, who passes the citizenship test and promises to be loyal to the United States

socialism a form of government in which the state owns all the property and businesses and people are paid according to the type of work they do

treaty an agreement between two or more countries

Bibliography

Antell, Rachel. "Ethiopian Jews
(or Beta Israel)." *Africana.com*
http://www.africana.com/Utilities/
Content.html?&../cgi-
bin/banner.pl?banner=Blackworld&../
Articles/tt_388.htm

Arizona Daily Star, Bilingual Education vs.
Immersion series
www.azstarnet.com/bilingual/

Asenta Magazine
http://home.att.net/~asenta/headlines.html

Asgedom, Mawi. *Of Beetles and Angels:
A True Story of the American Dream.*
Chicago: Megadee Books, 2001.

Ashabranner, Brent.
The New African Americans.
North Haven, CT: Linnet Books, 1999.

Bailey, Donna, and Anna Sproule. *Philippines.*
Austin, TX: Steck-Vaughn, 1991.

Barnett, Jeanie M. *Ghana.*
Philadelphia: Chelsea House, 1999.

Bhalla, Nita. "Ethiopia's Forgotten Crisis,"
BBC News, 8/6/02
http://news.bbc.co.uk/1/hi/world/africa/2175923.stm
"Happy New Year 1993," *BBC News,*
9/12/2000
http://news.bbc.co.uk/hi/english/world/africa/
newsid_921000/921815.stm

Brill, Marlene Targ. *Guyana.*
Chicago: Children's Press, 1994.

Canadian Museum of Civilization.
"Mystery of the Maya"
http://www.civilization.ca/civil/maya/
mminteng.html

Catholic Answers
www.catholic.com

Cisternas, Carlos.
"US Dollar Becomes Ecuador's
Currency." *Associated Press,* 9/12/2000
www.globalpolicy.org/nations/dollar/
ecuador.htm

Citizenship and Immigration Canada.
"Cultural Profiles Project: Haiti"
http://cwr.utoronto.ca/cultural/english/
haiti/spirit.html

Cusick, Heidi Haughy.
Soul and Spice: African Cooking in the Americas.
San Francisco: Chronicle Books, 1995.

Danquah, Meri Nana-Ama, ed.
*Becoming American: Personal Essays by
First Generation Immigrant Women.*
New York: Hyperion, 2000.

Darwin Foundation
www.darwinfoundation.org

Doyle, Mark. "Rawlings: A Hard Act to
Follow." *BBC News,* 1/2/01
http://news.bbc.co.uk/1/hi/world/
from_our_own_correspondent/1097628.stm

Ecuador Explorer
www.ecuadorexplorer.com/html/
ecuador_food.html

Embassy of Ecuador
www.ecuador.org/index.htm

English, Merle. "Rags to Riches: He
Delivered. *Newsday,* 12/12/98
www.messengers.org/messville/
newsdy98.htm

Evolution
www.pbs.org/wgbh/evolution/

Exploring Religions, sponsored by the
Religious Studies Program at the
University of Wyoming
http://uwacadweb.uwyo.edu/religionet/er/
default.htm

Federation of American Scientists.
"Operation Safe Border"
http://www.fas.org/man/dod-101/ops/
safe_border.htm

Fernandes, Naresh. "Chutney: The Spice of
Life." *culturefront online,* New York Council
for the Humanities, vol. 6, no. 3
www.culturefront.org/culturefront/
magazine/98/winter/article.6.html

Financial Times. "Latin America:
Color My Money Green," 2/26/01
www.globalpolicy.org/nations/dollar/green.htm
"Mixed Blessing: Can Dollarized Ecuador
Avoid the Argentine Trap?" 1/24/02
www.globalpolicy.org/nations/dollar/
0124ecuador.htm

Foley, Erin L. *Ecuador.* New York:
Marshall Cavendish, 1995.

Ghana HomePage
www.ghanaweb.com/

Gish, Steven. *Ethiopia.* New York:
Marshall Cavendish, 1996.

Grant, Rosamund.
Caribbean and African Cooking.
Northampton, MA: Interlink Books, 1998.

Greenberg, Keith Elliot. *A Haitian Family.*
Minneapolis: Lerner Publications, 1998.

Guyana in Pictures. Minneapolis:
Lerner Publications, 1988.

Guyana: Land of Six Peoples
www.landofsixpeoples.com/gynewsjs.htm

Hadden, Jerry.
Teenage Refugees from Guatemala Speak Out.
New York: Rosen Publishing, 1997.

Hafner, Dorinda.
I Was Never Here and This Never Happened.
Berkeley, CA: Ten Speed Press, 1996.

Hultman, Tami, ed.
African News Cookbook: African Cooking for Western Kitchens. Africa News Service,
Penguin Books (Viking Press)
http://www.sas.upenn.edu/African_Studies/
Miscellany/Recipes_from_12913.html)

Israel Association for Ethiopian Jews.
"The History of Ethiopian Jews."
Jewish Virtual Library
http://www.us-israel.org/jsource/
Judaism/ejtime.html

Katz, Ian. "Greenback Magic?"
Business Week, 3/27/2000
www.globalpolicy.org/nations/dollar.htm

Kennedy, Danielle. "Top Entrepreneurs Share
Their Hottest Sales Pointers."
Entrepreneur.com 1996 (reprinted from
Seven Figure Selling (Berkeley Press)
http://www.entrepreneur.com/Magazines/
Copy_of_MA_SegArticle/0,4453,228838----
1-,00.html)

Kim, Hyung-chan, ed. *Distinguished Asian
Americans: A Biographical Dictionary.*
Westport, CT: Greenwood Press, 1999.

Kugel, Seth. "Neighborhood Report:
Jackson Heights; More Than Ever,
Ecuador Is Doing Business Here."
New York Times, 6/30/02.

Library of Congress Country Studies
http://memory.loc.gov/frd/cs/cshome.html

Lim, Silvio. "Obo Addy: Ghanian American
Drummer/Leader"
http://arts.endow.gov/artforms/Folk/
Addy.html

Malone, Michael. *A Guatemalan Family.*
Minneapolis: Lerner Publications, 1996.

Maya Paradise
www.mayaparadise.com

Miller, Trudy, and Andrew Miller.
A Human Rights History of Guatemala
http://www.west.net/~tmiller/gh/

Murray, Caryn Eve. "Courier Finds Right
Avenue." *Newsday,* 10/6/96
www.messengers.org/messville/
nyc-courierco.html

National Endowment for the Arts. 1999
National Heritage Fellowships in the Folk
and Traditional Arts. "Frisner Augustin,
Haitian Master Drummer"
arts.endow.gov/explore/Heritage00/August
inBio.html

Navarro, Mireya. "Guatemalan Army Waged
'Genocide,' New Report Finds."
New York Times, 2/26/99
http://www.globalexchange.org/campaigns/
guatemala/1999/navarro0226.html)

New Human Ancestor Found in Ethiopia
www.infoplease.com/ipa/A0779258.html

Noel's Pilipino Folkdance Glossary.
"Muslim/Moro Suite"
http://pw1.netcom.com/~ntamayo/
muslim.html

NOVA Online Adventure. *Tracking El Nino*
http://www.pbs.org/wgbh/nova/elnino/

O'Boyle, Lily Gamboa. *Pacific Crossings.*
New York: Acacia, 1994.

Peace Corps. "Kids World"
www.peacecorps.gov/kids/like/
ecu-celebration.html

Posadas, Barbara M. *The Filipino Americans.*
Westport, CT: Greenwood Press, 1999.

Public Broadcasting Corporation.
"Confronting the Legacy of the African
Slave Trade." *The Slave Kingdoms*
http://www.pbs.org/wonders/fr_e3.htm
"Ethiopia: An Ancient Legacy of
Christianity." *The Holy Land*
http://www.pbs.org/wonders/Episodes/Epi4/
holy_2.htm

Rabbit in the Moon
www.halfmoon.org

Riding, Alan. "Guatemala Guerrillas
Drawing Indians into Ranks for the First
Time." *New York Times,* 1/28/80.

Rumbaut, Ruben G., and Alejandro Portes,
eds. *Ethnicities: Children of Immigrants in
America.* Berkeley: University of California
Press, 2001.
Immigrant America: A Portrait. Berkeley:
University of California Press, 1996.
Legacies: The Story of the Second Generation.
Berkeley: University of California
Press, 2001.

Saywack, Rajendra.
"From Caroni Gyal to Calcutta Woman:
A History of East Indian Chutney Music
in the Caribbean," 12/99
www.guyanaundersiege.com/Cultural/
Chutney%20Music%20.htm

Schnapper, LaDena.
"The Ethiopian Coffee Ceremony"
http://buyethio.com/ethiopian_coffee_
ceremony.htm
Teenage Refugees from Ethiopia Speak Out.
New York: Rosen Publishing, 1997.

Serrill, Michael S., and Laura Lopez. "Hard-Luck President: Duran Ballen's Grand Plan for Modernization Has Fallen Apart, and a Nation Rues the Cost of His Failure." *Time,* 12/11/95 http://www.time.com/time/international/1995/951211/ecuador.html

Sheehan, Sean. *Guatemala.* New York: Marshall Cavendish, 1998.

Smithsonian Center for Folklife and Cultural Heritage. Articles from the 1997 Festival of American Folklife Program Book: African Immigrant Folklife www.folklife.si.edu/CFCH/97fest/1997progbook.htm

Aluko, Remi, and Diana Sherblom. "Passing Culture on to the Next Generation: African Immigrant Language and Culture Schools in Washington, D.C."

Belanus, Betty J. "Nile Ethiopian Ensemble: Profile of an African Immigrant Music and Dance Group."

Cook, Nomvula Mashoai, and Betty J Belanus. "A Taste of Home: African Immigrant Foodways."

Macharia, Kinuthia (researcher). "African Immigrant Enterprise in Metropolitan Washington, D.C.: A Photo Essay."

N'Diaye, Diana Baird. "African Immigrant Culture in Metropolitan Washington, D.C.: Building and Bridging Communities."

Nyang, Sulayman S. "Islamic Celebrations in the African Immigrant Communities in Washington, D.C."

Ofori-Ansa, Kwaku, and Peter Pipim. "Nature and Significance of Durbar in Ghanaian Societies."

Stabile, Tom. "Threads of the Imagination: How Africa's Kente Cloth Wraps around the World." *Humanities,* 7-8/98, online at National Endowment for the Humanities http://www.neh.fed.us/news/humanities/1998-07/kente.html

Stevens, John. "Majority Opinion—Sale v. Haitian Ctrs. Council, 113 S. Ct. 2549, 113 S. Ct. 2549, 125 L. (92-344), 509 U.S. 155 (1993)." Supreme Court of the United States, 6/21/93 http://supct.law.cornell.edu/supct/html/92-344.ZO.html

Stewart, Gail B. *Ethiopia.* New York: Crestwood House, 1991.

Takaki, Ronald. *In the Heart of Filipino America.* New York: Chelsea House, 1995.

Strangers at the Gates Again: Asian American Immigration After 1965. New York: Chelsea House, 1995.

Taste of Panama: History of the Panama Hat http://www.gdhq.com/ecuador/hat.html

Taylor, Robert. "Guatemala: Stubborn Stain of Corruption." *World Press Review Online* 6/02 www.worldpress.org/Americas/552.cfm

Tekavec, Valerie. *Teenage Refugees from Haiti Speak Out.* New York: Rosen Publishing, 1995.

Turck, Mary. *Haiti: Land of Inequality.* Minneapolis: Lerner Publications, 1999.

U.S. Agency for International Development www.usaid.gov

U.S. Census Bureau. Current Population Reports, Series P23-206. *Profile of the Foreign-Born Population in the United States: 2000.* Washington, DC: U.S. Government Printing Office, 2001.

U.S. Central Intelligence Agency. *The World Factbook 2001* www.odci.gov/cia/publications/factbook/

U.S. Immigration and Naturalization Service. "This Month in Immigration History: November 1991" http://www.ins.usdoj.gov/graphics/aboutins/history/nov91.htm

Virtual Galapagos http://www.terraquest.com/galapagos/

Vodun (and related religions) www.religioustolerance.org/voodoo.htm

Voices of New York www.nyu.edu/classes/blake.map2001/

Wark, Andrew. *Who Was the Queen of Sheba?* 9/12/2000 www.ucalgary.ca/unicomm/NewsReleases/queenwho.htm

Watts, Richard. "Francois Duvalier." *Africana.com* http://www.africana.com/Utilities/Content.html?&../cgi-bin/banner.pl?banner=Blackworld&../Articles/tt_1035.htm

Weiner, Tim. "Guatemalan Leaders Covered Up American's Killing, U.S. Decides." *New York Times,* 3/24/96.

Westheimer, Ruth, and Steven Kaplan. "Surviving Salvation." *One World Magazine* http://www.oneworldmagazine.org/focus/etiopia/falash.html

Wings and Wheels: The Guyana Express http://www.nyc24.com/issue02/story02/page04.asp

Index